THE
UNCOOK
BOOK

THE UNCOOK BOOK

The Essential Guide to a Raw Food Lifestyle

TANYA MAHER

HAY HOUSE

Carlsbad, California • New York City • London • Sydney
Johannesburg • Vancouver • Hong Kong • New Delhi

First published and distributed in the United Kingdom by:
Hay House UK Ltd, Astley House, 33 Notting Hill Gate,
London W11 3JQ
Tel: +44 (0)20 3675 2450; Fax: +44 (0)20 3675 2451
www.hayhouse.co.uk

Published and distributed in the United States of
America by:
Hay House Inc., PO Box 5100, Carlsbad, CA 92018-5100
Tel: (1) 760 431 7695 or (800) 654 5126
Fax: (1) 760 431 6948 or (800) 650 5115
www.hayhouse.com

Published and distributed in Australia by:
Hay House Australia Ltd, 18/36 Ralph St,
Alexandria NSW 2015
Tel: (61) 2 9669 4299; Fax: (61) 2 9669 4144
www.hayhouse.com.au

Published and distributed in the Republic of South Africa by:
Hay House SA (Pty) Ltd, PO Box 990, Witkoppen 2068
info@hayhouse.co.za
www.hayhouse.co.za

Published and distributed in India by:
Hay House Publishers India, Muskaan Complex, Plot No.3,
B-2, Vasant Kunj, New Delhi 110 070
Tel: (91) 11 4176 1620; Fax: (91) 11 4176 1630
www.hayhouse.co.in

Distributed in Canada by:
Raincoast Books, 2440 Viking Way, Richmond, B.C. V6V 1N2
Tel: (1) 604 448 7100; Fax: (1) 604 270 7161
www.raincoast.com

Text © Tanya Maher, 2015

Photography © Charlie McKay, 2015

Publisher Michelle Pilley
Commissioning editor Amy Kiberd
Managing editor Julie Oughton
Project editor Salima Hirani
Art direction Charlie McKay
Senior design manager Leanne Siu Anastasi
Project designer Luana Gobbo

The information given in this book should not be treated as
a substitute for professional medical advice; always consult a
medical practitioner. Any use of information in this book is
at the reader's discretion and risk. Neither the author nor the
publisher can be held responsible for any loss, claim or damage
arising out of the use, or misuse, of the suggestions made, the
failure to take medical advice or for any material on third party
websites.

A catalogue record for this book is available from the British
Library.

ISBN: 978-1-78180-564-0

Printed and bound in Italy

Contents

Introduction

I discovered raw food not because I had a plethora of illnesses and this was my last resort. There was nothing wrong with me. I was fit, my body was in top shape, I never had to worry about what I ate, my parents were knowledgeable in alternative therapies, I had an awesome job in property, I was young, popular, invincible – I was healthy. Or so I thought.

Looking back at my life now, I can only picture a young girl living in complete denial. I often ate a tub of ice cream or an entire block of chocolate instead of lunch and dinner, because I figured I should choose one to avoid overeating. I partied 'til dawn in clouds of second-hand smoke and thought of it as the best form of exercise. I thought sleep was overrated. My whole back was covered in repulsive acne, but who cares because I couldn't see behind me and at the beach, it was easy to just sunbathe lying on it. I would often get knife-piercing pain in my stomach, but I was the best long-distance runner I knew, so it didn't matter. I didn't like my own reflection, but I could always grin or pull faces in photos to disguise what I thought was too round a face and too big a nose. I would be bedridden whenever the seasons changed, but so was everyone else, so there was nothing wrong. I even thought that a reflexologist who told me to change my diet immediately to save myself from emerging diabetes was mad because, surely, diabetes was only for people who were overweight? And while others would turn to binging when it came to work- or relationship-related stress, I considered myself lucky for losing interest in eating when I was stressed, because I starved and got slimmer.

It took me a long time to unlearn these stories I'd been telling myself. It took me even longer to realise how well I'd mastered blocking out what needed attention, because of how well I'd blocked out one particular major event in my life...

The year 1998 was one to remember. I survived my first year as a teenager, my first year in high school was almost over, my Russian accent had begun to sound more Kiwi (believe me, a foreign accent is a big deal when you are an immigrant at school) and, for the first time, I was allowed to go away with my best friend for our joint birthday celebrations. It was a rainy day, the road was long and winding, but it didn't matter because it was school holidays, I was with my bestie, we had lollies, hip-hop music to sing along to and the whole back of the car to ourselves. Nothing was going to stop us from laughing and dancing, not even a safety belt that straps you tightly to your seat. We both pulled our seatbelts over our shoulders and under our arms, so were secured only around our waists. The next thing I remember is seeing a four-wheel drive head on, an unimaginable strike of sharp pain in my abdomen, followed by our car quickly filling with smoke and the struggle to open a jammed door, because I couldn't possibly stay in a car that might blow up like in the movies.

I still have no idea whether it was five minutes or five hours between the car accident and being rushed to Auckland City Hospital by helicopter, although I do remember how fast the emergency crew chopped open my favourite checked blue trousers. And amidst the uncontrollable shivering of my entire body, the excruciating pain through my stomach to my back, the haunting repetition of ambulance crew voices shouting something about a fractured spine, I still managed to wish that I was wearing better underwear.

Everyone in both vehicles survived the crash, but no one walked away injury free. I broke my back and had to wear a full-body brace for four months. I still have a metal plate and screws joining my lower spine. My stomach was so badly bruised and swollen from the seatbelt (which also saved my life) that doctors proposed to remove my pancreas. To make this hospital stay even more memorable, a catheter burst inside me, spreading an infection through my bladder, all while I was being pumped with an intense dose of morphine, to which my body reacted with painful hives.

My mum and dad went through so much stress and my entire focus turned to recovery, just to see these two favourite faces laughing again. I tried hard to be a good girl and eat the mashed potato, ice cream and jelly they provided as hospital food but my body would not keep them in. I remember being so angry at it for spewing up anything that went in. My weight declined, as did all interest in food, until I couldn't tolerate the thought of it. Meanwhile, doctors were still waiting on my parents' decision on whether or not to remove my pancreas. Knowing that it was a key gland for proper digestion and hormone regulation, my wise family were determined to keep it intact.

We wanted to learn how to help my body to heal, but no one even knew about Google then, and raw food books certainly weren't known of in the library, so we did what came naturally in a moment of despair – we used intuition. Mum and Dad asked me to imagine different foods and name those that didn't immediately make me feel nauseous. There were so many foods I craved, I was literally starving, but the only ones I could entertain the idea of actually keeping in were peppermint tea, high-factor manuka honey and liquidized vegetables. How clever our bodies are. Even in the most vulnerable state, they know exactly what they need to survive. I know now that my body, being so inflamed and sensitive, asked specifically for peppermint tea for its soothing properties, manuka honey for its antiviral, antibacterial and antifungal protection from hospital bugs, and raw carrot juice for its antioxidants, nutrients and enzymes, to support my healing pancreas. My body knew that raw foods have the power to heal, it knew exactly which foods had the right nutrition for this healing and it was because of raw foods that I got to keep my pancreas – although I didn't even realise it at the time.

Fast forward 10 years and it was, again, Mum and Dad who inspired me to tap into that intuition and discover a calling within me so deep, it would bring positive meaning to all unfortunate past events. They read raw food expert Victoria Boutenko's books and literally changed their entire diet overnight. They got rid of the microwave, espresso machine and all the food in their pantry. They filled clear kitchen benches with alien equipment, the refrigerator with so much colour it looked like a kaleidoscope, and started dehydrating flax crackers as if they were stocking up for 21 December 2012. It was awesome to see them so enthusiastic about a diet, but it's not like I was about to start doing the same. After all, as you've heard, there was nothing 'wrong' with me. It was also around this time that my husband, Elliot, and I started dating, and I was more interested in showing off my cooking repertoire than rolling energy balls. But my curiosity was already ignited. I watched my parents shed weight, start to look younger, glow from within, sleep less and do more exciting things with their days, all with an enormous amount of energy and enthusiasm. I had to get my hands on that book!

It was when I read Victoria Boutenko's book *Green for Life* and her collection of testimonials from people who had reversed all manner of illnesses (from diabetes, heart conditions, obesity, asthma, chronic fatigue and cancer) with raw food that I made an important connection – that I had also healed my body, all those years ago, with raw food. It also occurred to me that if we can heal disease with raw food, surely we can prevent it, too. Now we're talking!

What I read in Boutenko's book made sense – as soon as you apply heat to foods, they shrivel up, vitamins and minerals diminish, antioxidants and proteins are halved and enzymes vital for digestion die entirely. Our bodies then spend all their efforts on digesting the mineral-depleted foods and leave us with little energy for anything else. What didn't make sense is why so few people knew about the raw power of plants. And in this I found my calling.

I immediately began making green smoothies for our breakfast. I loved to cook and experiment with foods, so was in no hurry to change our meals, but my taste buds began to long for more greens throughout the day. Without even thinking about it, I reached for a salad instead of a sandwich at lunchtime and filled half our dinner plates with fresh raw vegetables. I thought I had really lost it the day I salivated over spinach at a supermarket and came home without commercial chocolate. I was loving the new flavours our fresh diet had to offer, as well as all the benefits I detected – increased energy, focus and intuition, glowing skin and sparkling eyes, healing acne, and strong hair and nails. Most of all, I loved how much fun I was having in the kitchen. With so much attention paid to feeling awesome, it wasn't until later that I realised how my painful stomach cramps never returned, my headaches had diminished, my teeth stopped getting cavities, and how flu and colds became a thing of the past.

I knew I couldn't keep this all to myself, so as soon as we moved to London, I went knocking on yoga centre and restaurant doors offering to run lunchtime classes, got kitted up with equipment, started blogging recipes, selling green smoothies and raw chocolate at market stalls, joined raw food networking groups and attended any health-related workshop I could find. I trained as a Holistic Health Coach, which brought me into contact with many clients. This allowed me to witness the countless benefits of raw foods among athletes, expectant mothers, young professionals and the newly retired. All of this lead to the establishment of Tanya's in Chelsea with my dear friends Linda and Andreas. The news of London's newest raw food restaurant and Europe's first superfood cocktail bar was so well received that we set up a sister café within six months! Since my first attempts at explaining to friends what a raw food coach does, I've seen the living plant-based cuisine grow immensely in popularity, just as vegetarianism and veganism did decades before it, to become something considered much more the norm, rather than a weird fad. The recipes in this book are among those that are most popular at Tanya's and most relied upon in my home, and now I can't wait for you to try them for yourself. Enjoy feeling this alive!

x *Tanya*

What is Uncooking?

Uncooking is getting back to basics, celebrating your health and rediscovering your youth via the freshest, cleanest, most nutritious plant-based wholefoods.

These foods include fruits, vegetables including green leafy vegetables and herbs, nuts, seeds, legumes, sprouted grains and beans, wild and indoor greens, edible flowers, algae and sea vegetables, superfoods, oils, fermented foods and teas, medicinal mushrooms, natural sweeteners and spices.

There's no baking, frying, boiling or microwaving involved. These foods have not been refined, denatured, canned or chemically processed. They are not heated above 48°C. They are often referred to as 'living' foods (which is the name I prefer). In principle, you can sprout a raw almond and then plant it in the ground to produce more almonds, so it is 'living'. You can't do the same with a roasted almond.

Enjoying a raw food lifestyle can be as straightforward as peeling a banana, but there's so much variety to delight in. With thousands of ways to juice, blend, sprout, ferment, marinate, activate, freeze, shape, chop, process, grate, spiralise, roll, dip, mix and dehydrate, raw food is scrumptious and fun to make.

Then why no cooking?

One of the toughest jobs your body has is to digest food. When we apply heat to food (specifically, anything above 48°C), we destroy its enzymes. When the temperature increases further (57°C and above), we destroy many vitamins and nutrients. Finally, when the temperature is even higher than that (as it is in all cooking), amino acids and antioxidants can diminish by 70 per cent. This leaves us with sad, nutritionally deprived meals and tired, nutritionally deprived bodies.

Raw food has an abundance of enzymes that are crucial for every bodily function, from walking to breathing to cell repair to digesting the food we eat at least three times a day. We ourselves are born with a little bank of enzymes, but if we then eat foods without the enzymes (i.e. cooked foods, in which the enzymes have been diminished), the result is akin to spending more than we can deposit. Soon enough, the body overworks itself by continually having to produce more enzymes for its metabolism and, in effect, exhausts all its energy, which slows digestion, accelerates the ageing process and invites disease. We go bankrupt.

But when we consume enzyme-rich 'living' foods, they practically digest themselves and aid in clearing toxins at maximum speed, naturally, leaving you with energy to spare for the things you love (family time, gardening, reading, rollerblading and simply feeling awesome).

Are there rules to being a raw foodie?

I'd like to think not or, at least, that the 'rules' don't feel like restrictions once you notice visible improvements to your skin, hair and nails and begin to feel more alive than ever. My ideas on what it means to be a raw foodie are as follows:

1. In general, raw foodism means eating uncooked plant-based vegan foods – so no animal foods.

2. You don't need to be 100 per cent raw to reap the rewards. Do what feels good to you, always include uncooked veggies and greens with your meals and call yourself 'high raw'. I like to stay away from labels, however, apart from 'healthy' or 'nutritarian' (someone choosing the most nutritious foods available to them at any time).

3. Raw foods are foods that have not been heated above 48°C, even within the processes of drying, dehydrating and high-speed blending.

4. Condiments, oils, teas, salts and spices are very much part of the raw foodist's lifestyle, but to ensure we are living the clean and fresh way, ensure they are not pasteurised or do not contain preservatives and choose cold-pressed, unpasteurised and 'extra virgin' products.

Seven Reasons to Love Raw Food

As raw food cuisine grows in popularity, it's hard to ignore its positive impact, not just on our lives but on the planet. Many doctors recognise food as medicine and scientists have proven that consuming living foods can prevent and reverse chronic disease. Then consider the global concerns – land and water conservation, greenhouse gas emissions, waste, pollution. Turning to a plant-based diet could save the planet.

It's a serious world out there, but you don't have to be. In fact, you can contribute to the positive changes just by celebrating your love for raw food. And there are many reasons why you can fall in love with a raw food diet:

Lots of energy It feels great to sleep less (but better) and have extra hours in your day to do the things you love while just feeling awesome. Did you know the enzymes in raw food can give you all that? Since cooking destroys 100 per cent of enzymes, your energy goes towards breaking down food (see opposite page), leaving you with very little for anything else. By eating living foods, you make life easy on your digestive system and it rewards you with energy!

Better digestion It's pretty much impossible to overeat when it comes to living foods – they are full of nutrients and the body knows when it is topped up on nutrients. This, of course, means your digestion is fully supported. It is easy to overeat cooked food, because your 'stop' and 'slow down' triggers are numbed by the vitamin- and enzyme-depleted meal. By the time you feel discomfort and can't fit in any more, you've already overeaten. The whole system becomes clogged, resulting in slow digestion, bloating and tiredness.

Your own home 'farmacy' A pantry full of raw foods is a medicine cabinet direct from the farm, but here's a fun fact. Every whole food has a 'pattern' that visually echoes a body organ or physiological function. This pattern acts as a signal to indicate which part of the body the food can benefit. For example, a walnut resembles a brain. We know walnuts help to develop over three dozen neurotransmitters for brain function. We also know that tomatoes and red peppers are important for blood and heart health. Here's the clue – cut one open and you'll see four chambers inside, just like in a heart! If you have a health issue, determine which foods resemble the afflicted body part. You'll be amazed to find how good those foods can be for your targeted area.

Crazy tasty Gone are the days of a raw food diet consisting of carrot sticks and lamb's lettuce. Even I can be fooled by the most beautiful, creative cupcakes, pizzas, cheesecakes, wraps, nut cheeses and chocolates that look and taste like their cooked competitors. Gourmet raw food has flavour and texture galore. Your taste buds won't know what hit them!

Easy to make Yes, it's true that you can go overboard with all the equipment out there for your raw kitchen, but let's not forget that this lifestyle is all about getting back to basics, decluttering, simplifying and returning to what is most natural. There are many recipes for salads, soups and smoothies that are so simple to make, and there are a thousand ways to make them without special equipment.

Happier everything Crunching on fresh raw vegetables gets your whole body excited. It starts with the jaw, which, through chewing, sends signals to your brain to produce the happy hormone, serotonin. So chew more, chew slower, chew consciously and remember to chew in the first place!

Better intuition The transformation the body and energy field experience as you clear out the old and fuel up with the new is amazing. Animals have strong instincts. They know when they are about to be killed. When we eat their flesh, the adrenalin circulating in their bodies prior to death is passed to us. When I stopped eating meat, I felt at one with all living creatures and my natural intuition became stronger.

Things I Wish I Knew

People turn to livings foods for many reasons – to heal a chronic illness or a tortured relationship with food, to detox, to support family members, because they believe a plant-based diet is natural, or feel compassion for animals and a desire to make a difference. Whatever your WHY may be, crystalise it in your mind and write it down to help you when times get tough. Below I have listed things that I, and other raw foodies I've worked with, wished we had known before getting started:

Eat dessert first If we gave the digestive system a three-hour break between a meal and dessert, both would be well digested. But we fill up on a main meal, then pile dessert on top, overfilling and confusing the body. The sugar in dessert sits there and begins to ferment and putrefy, causing yeast and candida to multiply. Many health complications are due to eating dessert on a full stomach. If you eat sweets first, the body can break down the sugar quickly. You then eat the meal peacefully without rushing to dessert. Even if you overeat, the meal sits on top and shields the sugar from yeast attack.

Why it's hard to give up cooked food Cooking turns energy-giving carbohydrates into caramelised sugar. Sugar is addictive, causing a dependency on cooked food. To kick sugar addiction, it is best to transition to raw foods slowly. Add raw salads to every cooked meal or natural sweeteners and fruits to all your raw sauces, soups and salad dressings.

No disease can develop in an alkaline body Uncooked fruits and vegetables are full of water, so are hydrating and alkalising. To find out where you sit on the pH scale, use litmus paper (available from pharmacies). A reading below 7 is acid. For balance, aim for a reading of 7.36 or above.

Chocolate is on the menu! Cocoa and cacao are different products, even though they come from the same tree. Cacao is what you are after. It's raw, unprocessed and is one of the highest sources of antioxidants and magnesium there is.

Soak nuts And dried fruit, for that matter (see also p.33). Soaking makes them easier on your digestion. But don't be put off your trail mix if the ingredients are not soaked – it is still a hundred times better for you than a packaged snack.

Plants can fill all your protein and calcium needs Sesame and poppy seeds contain more calcium than dairy products. Make milk with them (see p.33), sprinkle them on salads and add them to a trail mix (see p.180). The most digestible form of protein is in green leafy vegetables – they contain all the essential amino acids your body needs.

You don't need all the equipment It's so easy to feel overwhelmed by kitchen gadgetry, but all you really need is a decent knife and a blender. Borrow one from a friend to 'try before you buy' or see my suggested list for the stage of the raw journey you're on at BetterRaw.com/shop.

Don't be afraid to be a nutritarian You are not joining a cult or signing a contract of no return. There's room for a little cooked sweet potato in your life – a nutritarian chooses the most nutritious foods available at any given time.

Winter is not only possible, it's awesome! It can be challenging to stick to raw foods when the weather turns cold. Simple things like adding extra spice, heating up your plates before serving, stirring hot water into raw soups and putting on an extra layer of clothes can make all the difference – and will keep you well immunised in winter.

Initial pains, headaches and discomforts are good Welcome to the detox club! Detox symptoms are normal (unlike toxins accumulating in your body and congesting your colon, kidneys and blood for years); they DO go away and then you feel reborn. When you experience detox symptoms, recognise the wonderful thing that you are doing for your body and celebrate every little sign of the health-destroying, disease-inviting toxins departing.

Getting the Nutrients

Living a perfectly balanced life and enjoying ideal health isn't only possible on raw foods, it's more likely – and more fun and more delicious, too.

The nutrients you get from raw foods are vital for wellbeing. Since you'll be getting such a bounty of them via the recipes in this book, it's good to be informed about nutrients that are often mistakenly thought to be absent in a raw food diet.

The one-and-only vitamin B12

Vitamin B12 is readily found in animal products. Deficiency in B12 is therefore common in those who don't eat animals and can lead to anaemia, heart disease, irreversible nerve damage, fatigue or complications in pregnancy. Everyone needs vitamin B12, but even if you are consuming meat and dairy, you can still be deficient, especially if you are over 50. Our bodies cannot produce vitamin B12 and are only able to store it for a few years, so supplementation is vital.

Some claim that vitamin B12 can be found in certain plant foods, but research shows that form is inactive and could even interfere with the absorption and metabolism of the active form. Fortified foods, such as nutritional yeast, offer a good source if taken regularly, but vitamin B12 is the largest vitamin and, because of its size, is very difficult to absorb orally. Your body makes a protein known as intrinsic-factor that binds with B12 in the stomach and helps it slide down the gut into your intestine to be absorbed. Vegan or not, if your body doesn't produce intrinsic-factor, it's easy to be deficient. The most reliable and bio-available form of B12 is methylcobalamin (not cyanocobalamin), supplemented through a transdermal patch or a sublingual spray.

The iron man/woman

Iron helps to carry oxygen to the body's tissues. Without oxygen, we won't be around for more than a few minutes. So, yeah – iron is pretty important. Anemia – iron deficiency – is common among children and women below 50 (who lose iron via menstruation), but taking too much iron (in the form of fortified foods and supplements) is not a good thing either – in abundance, it can oxidise and damage tissues in your body, leading to even more serious conditions. If this is all too confusing, your doctor can give you a serum ferritin test to identify the amount of stored iron in your body.

If your iron levels are too high, lower them by donating blood. If your iron levels are too low, obtain naturally occurring iron from these plant-based foods:

Algae Chlorella and spirulina are among the highest superfood sources.

Seeds Especially pumpkin and sesame seeds, but also sunflower seeds, flaxseeds and buckwheat.

Nuts All nuts contain a similar quantity of iron.

Legumes Try peas, beans, peanuts, lentils and other pulses.

Dark green leafy vegetables Especially spinach, kale, swiss chard, beetroot tops, rocket and watercress.

Dried fruits Try raisins, prunes, apricots and figs.

Dark chocolate Try raw dark chocolate and cacao powder.

The sunshine on vitamin D

Every cell and tissue needs vitamin D to thrive. Deficiency can lead to bone density loss, weak tissues, heart conditions, rapid ageing, reduced immunity and cancer. But 85 per cent of us are deficient without even knowing it. All you need to do is roll up your sleeves and face the sun for 10–15 minutes per day and your skin will produce this vitamin naturally. Since you'll be eating more raw, mineral-rich foods, you'll want to ensure that they are getting absorbed properly and vitamin D helps with that. If you are struggling to make it out into the sun or if you're overweight, dark-skinned, pregnant or elderly, look for a vitamin D3 mouth spray. Adding vitamin K2 supplement can help to balance D3 even more, prevent toxicity and even whiten your teeth.

The fermented-foods pro

Probiotics and, particularly, cultured vegetables are crucial to the functioning of many bodily functions, from digestion and detoxification to a strong immune system. The word 'probiotic' means 'promoting life', because these active, live bacteria live in a healthy person's intestinal tract, assisting in the absorption of nutrients, minerals and vitamins. They are sometimes referred to as 'healthy gut flora'. There are many factors that cause their destruction – poor diet, stress and taking antibiotics. This could result in threatening side effects, so it's vital that we give probiotics serious attention.

Although there are many yogurts and other animal products enriched with probiotics (often seen as 'includes *Acidophilus* and *Bifidus*), they don't always reach the gut alive. The best way to ensure you stay in top health and enjoy the best digestion without bloating is to ferment your foods (see the recipes for Sauerkraut, p.64, or Creamy Cultured Cheese, p.163). If you don't like the flavour of fermented foods, you can take capsules.

No single probiotic supplement works for everyone, but over his years in clinical practice, natural health expert Dr Joseph Mercola has established that most individuals respond more positively to *Lactobacillus sporogenes* than any other probiotic, so that is a great place to start. The live cultures count of the product you select should be in billions; the information should be on the product label.

The skinny on fats

A stroll around supermarket aisles is enough to confirm our cultural obsession with fat-free and low-fat foods. The multi-billion dollar diet industry is very good at reminding us that eating fat equals getting fat. I would vouch for the statement when it comes to anything containing trans fats (the 'bad fats'), but the 'good fats' (see below) haven't been called good for no reason. They will help nutrients to glide to your cells and aid in digestion, they will oil your joints, protect your heart, improve your focus (the brain is 60 per cent fat), slow absorption so you can go longer without feeling hungry and even carry fat-soluble vitamins A, D, E and K to help release stored fat.

I can't imagine a world without the skin-glowing, hair-shining avocado, but when its fat and calorie content shows up identical to a highly processed, carcinogen-filled hot dog, I don't need scientific proof to tell me that not all fats are equal. Include more of the good fats in your diet. These lists will help you find the best sources:

Monounsaturated fats Olive oil and olives, avocados, nuts (almonds, macadamia nuts, hazelnuts, pecans, cashews), peanuts. Warning: although this fat is found in many other oils, if they are not 'extra virgin' (raw), they have been hydrogenated and bleached and have become trans fats.

Polyunsaturated fats Omega 3 and Omega 6 fats are both in this category and are absolutely crucial to the body in the fight against Alzheimer's, heart disease, poor concentration, depression and bad skin. The challenge is to eat them in equal portions, but the reality is that 15 times more Omega 6 is consumed (vegetable oils, margarine, ready meals, etc.). I recommend you shift your focus entirely to Omega 3 and eat foods containing these fats in abundance, because the chances are you are getting enough Omega 6 in your diet.

Another dietary challenge is to obtain all three components of Omega 3s – ALA (found in algae, flaxseeds and walnuts, and chia, sunflower, hemp and pumpkin seeds), EPA and DHA (both found in cold-water fish and fish oil). EPA and DHA are especially vital for pregnant and nursing mothers. Fish are now highly contaminated with toxic mercury, so if you are consuming animal products, choose krill oil. Vegetarians can take spirulina and chlorella, a form of ALA most efficient at converting to EPA and DHA.

Saturated fats These are often labelled 'bad fats', because of sources such as pork and ice cream, which make the original 'good fats' ineffective by processing, cooking and being turned to trans fats. The only option should be coconuts and coconut oil, but look for extra virgin products.

The calcium question

Dairy milk, once upon a time, came from happy, free range cows. They needed no hormone injections or antibiotics, the milk didn't require pasteurisation or homogenisation and, with the simple diet we once ate, the quality and quantity of dairy we consumed didn't interfere with digestion. It's not a topic I enjoy bringing up, but we've gotta get with the times and take responsibility for our health and our planet. It is true that cows' milk was and is still rich in calcium and other nutrients – it is, after all, designed to develop calves. But we share no anatomical similarities with calves and have no evolutionary relationship with them. Calcium in dairy is wrapped in casein (used in industrial glue and paint thickener). Calves easily split casein using rennet, an enzyme produced in their stomachs, but humans produce rennet only during the first month of their lives.

Not to worry. Here are some foods that contain calcium in a more bio-available form than dairy foods, and that provide even more nutrients and minerals for superhuman bones, muscles, nerves, hair, nails, heart and blood:

Seeds Poppy seeds contain more calcium than any other plant source and any animal source, too (see Calcium Sunrise shake on p.35 for details). Sesame seeds are a close second, as calcium is found in tough, hard things, like seeds.

Nuts All nuts contain calcium, but almonds and Brazil nuts lead the way by miles.

Green leafy vegetables Collard greens, kale and turnip greens are particularly high in calcium. Spinach has plenty, too, but because its high oxalic acid content binds with the calcium, it makes the calcium less bio-available.

Sea vegetables Nori, kombu, agar-agar and, in particular, wakame are good sources of calcium.

Vegetables Many vegetables deliver calcium, but fibrous vegetables, such as cabbage and broccoli, are particularly rich sources.

Fruit Figs, olives and apricots are good sources of calcium.

Protein myths

Proteins are constructions of amino acids, which our bodies require to function properly. They are needed for cell growth and repair and maintaining all body tissues, such as skin, muscles and organs. I like to think of a protein molecule as a bead necklace consisting of 22 beads (amino acids). Our bodies can make 13 of these, but the other nine are essential, meaning that we need to put them into our bodies via the foods we eat. Some people claim that animal products are the only sources of these essential amino acids and that you need a lot of protein, but that is not true. To test this theory, look to nature for clues. We require protein the most during infancy and childhood, when we experience rapid physical growth, and breast milk contains approximately 1g of protein per 100ml. Considering what newborns drink, we are talking 1–8g of total daily protein intake. It's confusing, then, that the daily recommended intake for adults is 50–60g. Another clue from nature is that large herbivores – cows, elephants, giraffes, horses and rhinos – are strong and live long lives.

Rest assured that you will not be short of protein in a raw food diet and will get all the essential amino acids if you eat at least one food from each of these categories:

Nuts Especially almonds, pistachios, cashews and walnuts.

Seeds Quinoa and buckwheat, both of which are mistaken for grains; sunflower, chia, pumpkin and hemp seeds.

Green leafy vegetables Especially if they are dark green.

Legumes Peanuts, beans, peas and lentils.

Superfoods Chlorella, spirulina, bee pollen and goji berries.

The soy issue

Many products in supermarkets are made of soya and corn (they are fed to cows, too, and even the lecithin in commercial chocolate comes from soya beans). The majority of soya and corn is genetically modified, and soya has the highest levels of contamination by pesticides of all foods. Soya also contains many enzyme inhibitors that slow down protein assimilation, causing digestive problems. Many people believe that cooking can help make foods that are difficult to digest a little easier on the system, but since soy is resistant to heat, cooking won't solve the issue (tofu, soy milk and yogurts are all cooked). The only thing that will reduce anti-nutrients (compounds that interfere with the absorption of minerals and nutrients) is long fermentation. You may read that tofu is a complete food with protein, calcium and iron, however there are so many issues with soy that unless it's fermented (miso, tamari and tempeh), I'd keep my distance.

Equipment

There are some pieces of kit that make preparing raw dishes a breeze. Who doesn't love a bit of gadget shopping? But many of the tools you need will be in your kitchen already.

Sure, the gadgetry all looks slightly alien (a dehydrator?) and sounds a tad odd (did you say 'nut bag'?), but it's only overwhelming if you try to buy the entire lot in one go. Let this be a fun process – look at your favourite raw food recipes to see which bits of kit appear in those most often. Now you have a good indication of what to invest in first.

The only thing you really need to get started is a good sharp knife. A beginner on a budget can still make over half of my recipes using just three tools – a nut bag, a knife and an all-in-one food processor (a combined food processor and blender with grating slicers, nut grinder and citrus juicer attachments – good brands are Kenwood and Philips).

Main appliances

If you enjoy gourmet raw cuisine, it's worth investing in these four key contributors.

Blender A liquidiser that will turn whole fruits, vegetables and nuts into smoothies, sauces, soups, ice creams and even nut butter. A high-speed blender with a powerful motor and sharp blades can break through cellulose cells in greens, making nutrients more available for us to assimilate when drinking smoothies. I highly recommend Vitamix. Other good brands include Blendtec and Omniblend.

Juicer A machine that pulverises fruits and vegetables to extract the juice and discard the pulp (fibre). There are two main types of juicer – centrifugal and cold-press:

Centrifugal This is a cheaper model, great for beginners and easy to clean, but it can damage vital nutrients and enzymes in your produce and is ineffective at juicing leafy greens and herbs. Decent brands include Breville, Philips and Kenwood.

Cold-press In a cold-press juicer, augers turn to gently crush produce (a process that is much like chewing). It is more costly than a centrifugal juicer and takes longer to extract juice, but it extracts more juice and the quality and nutrient content is exceptional, so if you juice often, you will save in the long run. I use Tribest's Green Star Elite at home and Norwalk at Tanya's Café. Other good brands include Hurom, Green Power and Angel.

Food processor A food processor offers the quickest and most effective way of combining whole ingredients without thinning with liquids, for making anything from cakes to nut butters. When you're ready to upgrade, go for one of the top brands – Cuisinart or Magimix. Both serve the same functions to chop, grate, mix, whisk and grind.

Blender

Cold-press juicer

Food processor

Dehydrator

Dehydrator An amazing machine that is about the size of a microwave oven and is raw food's version of an oven. A dehydrator slowly removes the moisture from produce, making it dense and chewy (think living breads, burgers, kale chips and granola), which is especially satisfying when you are transitioning from cooked food. It works at very low temperatures so the nutritional and enzyme content are not jeopardised. Excalibur is the ideal basic model and all you need is a five-tray dehydrator to get started. I use Tribest's Sedona nine-tray model, which can be divided into two drying chambers and has a quiet night-time mode. Whichever type you go for, remember to buy Teflex sheets, which do the same job in a dehydrator as baking paper does in an oven. You'll need them for making fruit leathers, crackers and pizza bases.

Main equipment
Below is a list of my absolute favourite kitchen tools:

Scales and volume-measuring tools These cost very little, but I use them all the time. Just remember to stock up on spare batteries.

Nut bag This multi-purpose straining bag can be used for making nut and seed milks, sprouting and even juicing, if you own a blender but not a juicer. It's possible to make nut milk using a sieve, cheese cloth or (clean!) stockings, but nut bags are easy to use and no longer difficult to find.

Knife A good sharp knife will change your life and it's essential as, on a raw food diet, you'll be chopping more fruits and vegetables than ever before. You don't need to spend a fortune on one and you can't go wrong with a Japanese brand. Just remember to get a sharpener to keep the blade well maintained.

Spiraliser A kitchen must-have if you like to have fun! The spiraliser is an absolutely awesome invention for making courgetti (courgette spaghetti), and for making vegetables fine and curly to spruce up your salads. I prefer standing models over horizontal ones, because they use the whole vegetable and don't waste the middle part. (You can see a picture of one of these on p.54).

Double boiler A double boiler is super handy when you need to melt cacao butter or coconut oil and want to ensure they don't cook or burn. I use a simple method of stacking a stainless steel bowl over a pan filled with hot water.

Mandoline This is one of my favourite gadgets for slicing veggies quickly and uniformly for that professional look. It's perfect for making vegetable lasagne sheets and cannelloni. I highly recommend you buy a microplane cut-resistant glove to protect your hands – mandoline blades are sharp!

Water purifier Every cell in the body needs water in order to function properly, and you'll be using plenty of it in nut milks, smoothies, cakes and soups. Tap water contains many nasties, from toxins and chemicals to heavy metals, which are important to avoid. I use the EVA Filtration System at home – it has the most complete filter cartridge system in Europe and produces the most delicious water.

Handy tools
You may already have some of these tools, which I list here starting with the most frequently used in my kitchen:

Nut grinder or mini travel blender
Chopping board
Rubber spatula
Lemon squeezer
Cleaver knife
Garlic press
Veggie peeler
Grater
Citrus juicer
Springform cake tins and loose-based tart tins
Chocolate moulds and cupcake cases
Piping bag
Jars and storage container
Mixing bowls
Pepper grinder
Sieve/strainer
Kettle
Boston shaker (for cocktails)
Sprouter
Ice cream maker

Stocking the Pantry (Shopping Time!)

When you are new to uncooking, not much looks or sounds familiar, and that's ok – you were once new to cooking, too. However, as you skim through the list of staple produce below, you'll notice that you already recognise all the food groups, and you may well find that there are more of them than you originally thought. Raw foods are abundant in variety. Let this fact excite you rather than overwhelm you.

There's no need to spend a fortune – stock up a little at a time. Begin by adding two or three items to your weekly grocery list and, in no time, you'll be equipped to make any recipe in this book. I've designed my recipes to use ingredients that are easily found in a supermarket or health food shop. Note that the further down this list an item appears, the more likely it is you'll need to look for it in a health food shop.

Nuts and seeds make up a major part of a raw food diet, so it's worth buying them in bulk. You can store them in the freezer – they will stay fresh for up to three years.

Fruits Lemons, limes, avocados, apples, oranges, bananas, watermelons, cantaloupe/rock melons, pineapples, berries (fresh and frozen), pears, kiwi fruits, nectarines, passion fruit, grapefruit, grapes, papaya, figs and coconuts (both mature brown and young green, which are sometimes mistakenly categorised as nuts).

Veggies Courgettes, celery, carrots, beetroot, sweet potatoes, mushrooms (oyster, button, chestnut, portobello, shiitake), asparagus, fennel, sweetcorn (fresh, frozen and baby corn), popped garden peas, mangetout, broccoli, cauliflower, cabbage, parsnips, Jerusalem artichokes, butternut squash or pumpkins and, of course tomatoes, cucumbers, aubergines and red, yellow, orange and green peppers (which are all fruits, but found in supermarket vegetable aisles).

Green leafies Kale, cavolo nero, spinach, romaine lettuce, chicory lettuce, watercress and rocket.

Herbs and wild edibles Mint, basil, parsley, thyme, coriander, dill, spring onion, chives, rosemary, snow pea and sunflower shoots, edible flowers (fresh and dried pansies or rose petals) and micro greens.

Nuts and seeds Nuts (almonds, cashew nuts, hazelnuts, walnuts, pecan nuts, Brazil nuts, pine nuts, pistachio nuts), seeds (sunflower, chia, sesame, pumpkin, poppy and hemp seeds, both hulled and in the shell), plus buckwheat and quinoa (both of which are mistaken for grains).

Grains and legumes Rolled oats (buy ready-sprouted porridge oats), sprouted mixed beans and lentils, alfalfa sprouts and bean sprouts.

Sea vegetables and algae Wakame, dulse, nori, kelp noodles, spirulina and chlorella.

Spices and flavourings Himalayan salt, peppercorns, garlic (fresh and powder), onion (fresh white and red onions, spring onions and onion powder), ginger (fresh and ground), turmeric, ground cumin, garam masala, paprika (plain and sweet smoked), cayenne pepper, chilli (fresh, powder and flakes), winter spices (ground cinnamon and sticks, nutmeg, coriander, star anise, cardamom), mixed Italian and other dried spices (dried basil, parsley, oregano, thyme, dill, rosemary, sage), caraway seeds, wasabi powder, Dijon mustard and vanilla (pod, extract and powder).

Fats, oils and butters Extra virgin coconut oil, extra virgin olive oil, toasted sesame oil (it's not raw, but so good you'll eat way more healthy salad with a dash of this), other oils (caster oil, hemp or flaxseed oil), raw tahini, almond butter, coconut butter, peanut butter (it's not raw, so use it only occasionally), cashew/macadamia nut butters and canned coconut milk (it's not raw – buy only organic with no additives).

Condiments Tamari or nama shoyu (both are fermented soy sauces), Bragg's liquid aminos, apple cider vinegar, balsamic vinegar, miso paste (sweet white and dark), nutritional yeast (look for a product that is fortified with vitamin B12), sundried tomatoes (preferably preserved in salt, but look for quality oil if preserved in oil), olives and Tabasco sauce.

Sweeteners Dried fruits (pitted dates, Medjool dates, raisins, apricots, pineapple, goji berries, mulberries, golden berries and desiccated coconut), maple syrup (it's not raw, but it contains minerals and has a beautiful flavour), agave nectar (a highly controversial ingredient, see also p.186), raw honey (one with a minimum of UMF 10+ is best), coconut palm sugar, xylitol, freeze-dried strawberries (or powder), yacon syrup and liquid stevia.

Superfoods Cacao (powder, butter, paste/liquor and nibs), matcha green tea powder, lucuma powder, maca powder, bee pollen, acai (powder and pulp), medicinal mushrooms (cordyceps, chaga, reishi), carob, algarroba and baobab.

Other Dairy-free probiotic capsules, Medicine Flower extracts (coffee, butterscotch or caramel and hazelnut), peppermint essential oil, coffee beans, Assam tea leaves (or English breakfast tea bags), coconut flour (or buckwheat flour), kombucha and rice papers.

Organic's the word

It's no secret that organic produce usually costs more than conventionally grown produce. I'm not thrilled about that either. But I know that if I ordered a salad topped with nuts and dressing, I didn't order a salad topped with nuts, dressing, pesticides, fungicides and a dash of herbicides! Organic produce tastes better and is more nutritious, because it is free of cancer-causing carcinogens and grew in richer soil. If pesticides destroy and blow up the stomachs of insects, and if we are just bigger versions of these living creatures, it stands to reason that the only difference between the impact of these chemicals on them and on us is time.

If the cost of switching to organic is a big jump for your family, start slowly and lower your pesticide intake by eating more of the Clean Fifteen (the 15 least contaminated products) and fewer of the Dirty Dozen (the 12 most contaminated products – try to buy only organic ones of these). You can get an updated list each year from ewg.org, or Google the terms for more information.

Clean Fifteen Avocados, sweetcorn, pineapples, cabbage, sweet frozen peas, onions, asparagus, mangoes, papayas, kiwi fruit, aubergine, grapefruit, cantaloupe, cauliflower and sweet potatoes.

Dirty Dozen Apples, peaches, nectarines, strawberries, grapes, celery, spinach, peppers, cucumbers, cherry tomatoes, snap peas and potatoes (and often kale and blueberries, too).

Eat the seasons

Seasonal foods are so much sweeter, tastier and more nutrient dense than any force-grown produce. Mother Nature is full of clues and inspiration for us to follow her cycle, as she provides us with an abundance of sweet fruits for endurance during ever-active summers and calming root vegetables for grounding, settling down and recharging during winters. Check EatTheSeasons.com for seasonal food lists.

Loco for local

When produce is flown halfway across the globe to ensure that our supermarket shelves look identical all year round, the effects go far beyond the environmental impact of this level of transportation. An apple may very well have been grown in the rich soils of my beloved New Zealand, but when it is picked too green and ripens unnaturally away from the tree during its lengthy journey to me in the UK, it loses a lot of its vital nutrition. Conventionally grown tomatoes are gassed to speed up ripening and apples are coated in toxic wax to look presentable. Eat organic, locally grown, seasonal foods to feel more intuitive, peaceful and connected with the earth, people, animals and yourself.

CHAPTER 1
Drinks

There's no better or faster way to deliver
nutrients to your system than with a glass
of fresh, energising liquid love. I use my blender
or juicer every single day and I even travel
with one. This chapter includes recipes for
my very favourite juices, smoothies, shakes
and hot drinks, many of which can replace an
entire breakfast or lunch because of how filling,
nutritious and satisfying they are.

Juices

— EACH SERVES 2

Start your day with a green juice and you've given yourself the best chance to meet the challenges ahead with vigour and vitality. If you're on a detox programme, juicing will be tremendously beneficial to your regime. To make the recipes here, simply pass the ingredients through a juicer. If you don't own a juicer, don't despair. There's no reason why you should miss out on all these nutrients – simply combine the ingredients in a blender, then strain the mixture through a nut bag.

TANYA'S TOP TIP

• *If you are not using organic fruits or vegetables, wash them in water mixed with apple cider vinegar. Slice them to fit your juicer chute and remove any stones. Juice and enjoy immediately.*

• *Pass softer ingredients through the juicer before hard ones (for instance, pears and strawberries before celery). If the soft items cause a build-up of purée in your juicer, push through a few hard items to clear the works.*

• *Pass leafy greens into the juicer before or with other veggies to avoid waste – if any leaves become stuck in the works, the other items will push them along.*

• *Fresh is always best. If you must make juice ahead of time, only make it for a maximum of 16 hours in advance to avoid it becoming heavily oxidised. Store fresh juice in an airtight glass container in the refrigerator.*

• *You can freeze your juice and defrost at a later stage, but note that it may lose 5–20 per cent of its nutrients. Avoid freezing it in glass, which can burst when the juice expands during freezing.*

Everyday Green

If an apple is picked when it is unripe (so it can travel to another country to be sold), it continues to develop away from the tree, with none of the benefits of soil and water, which means nutrients cannot multiply. Furthermore, the carbohydrates become sugars, making the apple unnaturally sweet. Eating local apples, soon after harvest, is the answer. Granny Smiths, which I use in this juice, are packed with antioxidants and are harvested in winter.

4 green apples, such as Granny Smith
4 celery sticks
1 large cucumber
300g (10½oz) kale, spinach or your
  favourite leafy greens
2.5–5cm (1–2in) root ginger
sunflower or snow pea shoots, to taste
  (optional)

Kidney Kicker

The kidneys are crucial to wellness because they help to process everything that goes into our systems, including alcohol, pesticides, processed foods and medicines. To support these vital organs in this huge responsibility, give them a break with this cleansing, easy-to-digest juice. All the ingredients help to boost kidney function and are easily processed.

3 green apples, such as Granny Smith
150g (5½oz) asparagus
4 celery sticks
2 lemons (with peel, if organic)
1 cucumber
fresh cranberries, to taste, when in
  season (optional)

Immunity Booster

All foods with dark pigmentation, such as berries, grapes and beetroot, contain high levels of antioxidants. Ginger has the power to fire up your digestive juices and promote healthy perspiration while also improving the absorption and assimilation of antioxidants. So with this juice, you don't just get the vital stuff in, you also get the bad stuff out.

1 beetroot
150g (5½oz) cherries, pitted
5 carrots
5cm (2in) root ginger
1 lemon

Tutti Frutti

I don't do diets, but if there was one to choose, I'd go down the fruitarian route. And then I'd pick my favourite fruits in the whole wide world and juice them all day long... On such a diet, this juice would be a regular for me.

200g (7oz) strawberries
1 large cucumber
½ cantaloupe melon, peeled and cored
½ pineapple, peeled and cored
2 pears

Skin Cleanser

When I was a child, watermelon was on tap. Dad would buy it when in season and there was always a cut melon in the kitchen, ready for us to help ourselves. Rich in vitamins A and C and antioxidants, and with a high water content, watermelon is great for radiant skin. This juice is a delicious way in which to take it.

720g (1lb 9½oz) watermelon, chopped together with skin
320g (11¼oz) strawberries
1 cucumber
½ red pepper
35g (1¼oz) alfalfa sprouts
small bunch of mint

The Healer

Turmeric's ability to reduce inflammation is well documented, but many other foods achieve the same results, including the other ingredients in this truly healing concoction.

5 carrots
1 sweet potato, peeled
½ fennel bulb
¼ pineapple, peeled and cored
handful of basil leaves
5cm (2in) fresh turmeric root (or 2 tsp ground turmeric)

Heavy Metal Detox

It's difficult to avoid exposure to heavy metals in today's world – they enter the body through food and water, as well as via the skin, which absorbs them from the air. We are lucky to have so many food sources of pectin, sulphur, antioxidants and enzymes that effectively remove mercury, cadmium, lead, uranium and aluminium from our systems. This juice will give you a blast of these beneficial nutrients.

30g (1¼oz) parsley
30g (1¼oz) coriander
100g (3oz) fresh garden peas
4 celery sticks
4 green apples, such as Granny Smith
280g (10oz) green grapes
1 courgette

Following pages, from left to right:
Work It Out (see p.35), Skin Cleanser (see above), Immunity Booster (see above), Choctastic (see p.34), Strawberries & Cream (see p.31), Love Your Liver (see p.31), The Healer (see above), Everyday Green (see opposite page), The Spiral (see p.30)

Juices Vs Smoothies

One of the most common questions I am asked is this: 'Which do you recommend – smoothies or juices?' The answer is simple: each constitutes an important part of a raw food diet, both play a key role in my wellness regime and I recommend you consume both juices and smoothies on a regular basis. So what's the difference? Smoothies and juices are prepared in different ways and, consequently, they deliver their goodness in different ways, as I outline below. This chapter includes recipes for juices, smoothies and shakes. Shakes are, in essence, smoothies that contain nuts and seeds. My smoothies are fruit and vegetable based, so are safe for anyone with nut sensitivities.

Equipment Smoothies are made in a blender (see p.18), which consists of a jug and a motor stand. Motor power affects the quality of the smoothie produced – the higher the power, the better the outcome. The blender's price usually directly correlates to smoothie quality and nutritional density.

Juices are made using a juicer (see p.18), which consists of various components that, together, separate the liquid (juice and nutrients) from the pulp (fibre) contained in vegetables and fruits. There are two main types of juicer. Centrifugal juicers use a high-speed spinning technique combined with shredding to separate juice from pulp. Cold-press (or masticating) juicers crush and press juice from the pulp. Juice made using a cold-press juicer has a higher nutritional content, as the spinning process of centrifugal juicers creates a little heat, which can destroy some nutrients.

Prep and clean time Whether using a blender or juicer, preparing fruits and veggies takes the same amount of time. Using a blender to make a smoothie or a centrifugal juicer to produce a juice takes roughly the same amount of time. Using a cold-press juicer is a considerably slower process.

Cleaning is the aspect that deters many from juicing. As a blender has only a jug and a lid to rinse, cleaning is speedy. With a juicer, you must take apart the various components, rinse them individually and scrub the filter to remove pesky fibres of pulp.

Fibre When you make a smoothie in a blender, you whizz up whole fruits and vegetables, resulting in a thick, smooth, creamy drink. You consume all the fibre contained in the ingredients, and as fibre releases energy slowly, a smoothie will keep you full and keep you going for longer than a juice.

Because fibre is removed in juicing, a juice is thinner than a smoothie. It makes a great thirst quencher and provides an instant energy boost.

Nutrients The organisation juicingscience.com commissioned the National Measurement Institute in Melbourne, Australia, in December 2013 to conduct laboratory tests to explore the nutritional differences between juices and smoothies made with the same ingredients. The results revealed that green juice made with a juice extractor contains up to twice the concentration of key nutrients of those ingredients blended in a leading commercial blender. Smoothies, however, retain more calcium, probably due to the fibre content.

Heat destroys nutrients and blenders create more heat than juicers. But even after one minute of blending, heat doesn't surpass 28°C, so there is never enough heat to cause significant vitamin or enzyme damage. The most relevant explanation here is that the oxidation (air pushing into cells) that occurs in blenders causes most nutrient damage.

Starting out If you've never tried a detox programme, I would suggest investing in a blender and adding daily wholefood smoothies to your diet to transition to a cleaner lifestyle. The fibre contained will slowly clear out your digestive tract and will keep you sated. Once your system is clean and strong, switch to juicing. Without the fibre, nutrients will be easily absorbed into your bloodstream for an immediate energy kick.

Smoothies

– EACH SERVES 2

Smoothies are a highly versatile part of the raw food diet, not to mention the fact that they are delicious and feel like a real treat – a creamy smoothie makes the perfect breakfast, brunch, lunch or energising snack between meals. You'll need to chop up all your fruits and vegetables before blending them, although with a high-powered blender, the chunks can be quite large.

TANYA'S TOP TIP

- *Buy your favourite fruits when they are in season, then deseed, peel, chop and freeze them. This way, you fill up your freezer, so it runs more efficiently, and you will always have supplies for making smoothies in an emergency or for lazy days.*

- *For the perfect green smoothie, pack your blender with fruits and green leafy vegetables in equal proportions.*

- *For a velvety drink, include a creamy fruit (try pear, banana, mango, papaya, avocado, young coconut or peach).*

- *Chlorophyll, found in green leafy vegetables, cleanses and alkalises the blood. Experiment with combinations of greens (try spinach, parsley, lamb's lettuce, romaine, sunflower or snow pea shoots, any green vegetable tops, wheatgrass, celery leaves and kale).*

- *Use a citrus press to obtain lemon, lime, grapefruit or orange juice for your smoothies. Use a juicer to obtain other fruit or vegetable juices.*

Shine So Bright

It's no secret that berries are high up on the list of foods that are full of antioxidants – the blueberry, after all, is the original superfood. And it's no secret that they are among the tastiest of foods, either! Fight off free radicals and get your skin glowing with this tempting drink.

250ml (8½fl oz) water
720g (1lb 9½oz) chopped watermelon flesh
50g (1¾oz) blueberries
55g (2oz) raspberries
4 strawberries
¼ avocado or 1 banana
1 tbsp acai powder
ice (optional)

Blend all the ingredients in a blender, pour and enjoy!

Tangy Passion

The ingredients of this fruity smoothie combine so beautifully in flavour, texture and colour that I find myself making it as often as I do a green smoothie. You'll hardly notice yourself downing a glassful of nutrients.

360ml (12¼fl oz) orange juice (juice of approximately 4 oranges)
120ml (4fl oz) water
2 kiwi fruits, peeled
1 ripe mango, peeled and stoned
1 banana, peeled, chopped and frozen
½ tsp ground turmeric
pulp and seeds from 2 passion fruits

Blend all the ingredients, except the passion fruit, in a blender until creamy, adding more water if necessary. To serve, pour the smoothie into glasses and top with the passion fruit pulp and seeds.

Savoury Green

This filling and refreshing smoothie is ideal for those who like their nutrients delivered in a savoury package. Kiwis contain twice the vitamin C of oranges, so your immune system is bound to celebrate.

4 kiwi fruits, peeled
3 handfuls of your favourite greens
3 celery sticks
½ avocado
juice of ½ lemon
1cm (½in) root ginger
½ ripe mango (optional)
water, as needed

Chop the fruits and greens, unless you have a powerful blender. Cover with water and blend. Make extra, as this juice keeps, refrigerated, for up to 4 days.

Sweet Green Goddess

Pineapple is one of the most delicious exotic fruits and its incredible thick skin protects the nutrients contained in the flesh for when you need their protection. The impressive roll call includes vitamin C, manganese, potassium and bromelain, which all help to reduce inflammation, suppress coughs and boost immunity, especially when taken with green leafy vegetables.

⅓ ripe pineapple, peeled and cored
1 ripe pear, chopped
2 nectarines, stoned
3 handfuls of greens
fresh mint leaves and banana (optional)
water, as needed

Chop the fruits and greens, unless you have a powerful blender. Cover with water and blend. Make extra, as this juice keeps, refrigerated, for up to 4 days.

The Spiral

Spirulina is a highly nutritious blue-green algae that is sold in powder form. In New Zealand, spirulina is also the name of a particular smoothie blend that is sold in many cafés, made of pineapple juice, banana and spirulina. Some people find this algae difficult to take, but want to benefit from its valuable properties; this delicious smoothie is the perfect way. Try it – it's a brunch favourite of mine.

500ml (18fl oz) apple juice (juice of approximately 5 apples – or use shop-bought cold-pressed apple juice)
240ml (8¼fl oz) water
2 bananas, peeled, chopped and frozen
150g (5½oz) pineapple, peeled and cored
2 tsp spirulina powder
2 tbsp coconut butter (optional)

Blend all the ingredients on a high speed setting, adding the coconut butter if you want a Greena Colada!

Sayonara Jet Lag

Whenever I travel, I still experience the same feelings of joy and excitement as my first time on a plane. No doubt that's the reason why I never get the jet-lag blues. Interestingly, I notice my body craves tomato juice only when I fly. I discovered that tomatoes contain melatonin, which helps control your sleep and wake cycles when they are thrown off their circadian rhythm. So whenever you are off on an adventure, choose foods that will increase your body's natural melatonin production, like this tasty smoothie.

½ ripe pineapple, peeled and cored
1 banana, peeled, chopped and frozen
juice of 4 oranges
2 tbsp jumbo oats
2 ripe tomatoes
140g (5oz) grapes
water, as needed
ice (optional)

Blend all the ingredients in a blender, pour and enjoy!

Love Your Liver

This drink is key to liver cleansing. Don't be put off by the idea of emitting garlic odour from your pores, which signifies a build-up of toxins in the body – the stronger the smell, the more toxins there are to eliminate. If you eat garlic often, you'll have fewer toxins and, therefore, less odour, allowing you to enjoy the benefits of this drink more often – it's the opposite of a vicious cycle!

240ml (8¼fl oz) orange juice (juice of 2–3 oranges)
240ml (8¼fl oz) grapefruit juice (juice of 1 large grapefruit)
120ml (4fl oz) water
4 tbsp caster oil or 80ml (3fl oz) extra virgin olive oil, hemp seed oil or flaxseed oil
4 garlic cloves
¼ avocado
2.5cm (1in) root ginger
½ tsp cayenne pepper, or to taste

Blend the ingredients until smooth. Drink slowly, ensuring each sip combines with your saliva for optimum digestion and cleansing.

Strawberries & Cream

There are no words to describe how much I adore this creamy dream of perfection, so I won't even try. Instead, I'll just dream about it and dribble over my keyboard as I type out the ingredients list.

250g (9oz) young coconut flesh (from approximately 2 young coconuts)
600ml (1 pint) coconut water (from approximately 2 young coconuts)
320g (11¼oz) strawberries
1½ bananas, peeled, chopped and frozen
2 tbsp agave nectar (optional)

Blend all the ingredients in a blender, pour and enjoy!

Making Nut or Seed Milk

I promise you I haven't met anyone who hasn't yet liked a seed milk the way I make it. The best-quality dairy is lovely because of its creamy texture and its flavour, which is slightly sweet and salty and a little umami. Use the recipe below to create your own perfectly balanced plant-based version.

Your choice of nuts or seeds: If you have American cup measures, use 2 cups nuts or 1½ cups seeds, or use 300g (10½oz) almonds, hazelnuts or Brazil nuts, 200g (7oz) walnuts, 280g (10oz) macadamia nuts, 220g (7¾oz) pecan nuts, 180g (6¼oz) sunflower seeds, 200g (7oz) hemp seeds, 210g (7¼oz) poppy seeds, 200g (7oz) pumpkin seeds or 160g (5¾oz) sesame seeds
1.5 litres (2½ pints) water
6-8 pitted dates, soaked for 4-6 hours
¼ tsp Himalayan salt

Put the nuts or seeds in a bowl and pour in more than enough filtered water to cover them. They will expand as they soak, so don't be shy – add extra water. Leave to soak overnight.

Rinse the nuts (give the water to your herbs and house plants – they thrive on it!). Transfer to a blender with the remaining ingredients and blend on a high speed setting for approximately 1 minute.

Strain the mixture into a jug or bowl through a fine sieve, nut bag, cheese cloth or non-coloured (and hopefully unused) stockings. Retain the pulp left in the sieve for making other recipes in this book. It can be kept, refrigerated, for up to 3 days. (Avoid using pulp containing hard-shell remains from unhulled hemp seeds or poppy seeds.) Transfer the milk to an airtight container and refrigerate for up to 5 days until ready to use. It will separate, so simply stir it before use.

Soak Your Seeds & Your Nuts!

Very few of my recipes call for dry nuts. In most cases, you'll notice I use nuts that have been soaked. So what's with the soaking?

Do you know anyone with nut sensitivities or have you experienced bloating after eating too many nuts? Most nuts and seeds contain enzyme inhibitors that stop us digesting them properly, so it's likely that the nuts are upsetting your tummy and also passing through your body undigested.

Mother Nature has many ways of protecting her offspring. In this case, nuts and seeds are her babies. She wants them to exit the body intact and find a nice fertile field in which to grow into healthy trees and plants. So she arms nuts and seeds with enzyme inhibitors. This situation is no good to us, though. If we want to make the most of what each nut or seed has to offer, soaking them to release the inhibitors is the way to go.

Soaking nuts and seeds makes them easier on the digestion, and on the blender, too. Their bitterness and acidity decrease and the nutrients and minerals they contain increase, like anything would during the activation stage towards sprouting.

Soak nuts overnight, or follow this general rule for minimum soaking times: 6-8 hours for tough nuts, such as almonds and hazelnuts; 4-6 hours for softer nuts and seeds, such as cashew nuts and sunflower seeds. You can leave nuts soaking for up to 3 weeks in the refrigerator. Simply rinse them every other day.

Shakes

— EACH SERVES 2

Smoothies made even creamier with nuts? What's not to like? Unless you are sensitive to nuts, these delicious drinks are full of body and flavour to provide a super-nutritious dairy-free treat. To make these recipes, combine the ingredients in a blender and serve immediately.

Endurance Boost

It wasn't until we moved to Europe that I got into skiing and we managed to go every season for six years. Even though we explored a different destination each time, I quickly learned that nutritious breakfasts were not to be found on the menu too easily, so I brought along a mini travel blender and ingredients that would travel well. The result was a shake so satisfying and energising it would keep me going on the slopes until well past lunchtime.

600ml (1 pint) water
1½ ripe bananas, peeled, chopped and frozen
2 tbsp manuka honey
2 tbsp Almond Butter (see p.109)
2 tbsp acai powder
2 tbsp bee pollen

Choctastic

You can use any non-dairy milk here, but there is something that's just so dreamy about the hazelnut and chocolate combination. If you would rather have a lighter drink, go for a seed milk and add a couple of drops of Medicine Flower hazelnut extract, so you can have all the nutritional benefits without compromising on taste.

500ml (18fl oz) hazelnut milk (see p.33)
2 ripe bananas, peeled, chopped and frozen
3 Medjool dates, pitted
3 tbsp cacao powder
½ tsp ground cinnamon
½ tsp vanilla powder (optional)

Pecan Pie in the Sky

I usually have the raw pecan pie ingredients to hand, so this is one of the shakes I like to whip out fast for visitors. It gets major praise from both raw lovers and sceptics, but my favourite feedback to date is this: 'I can't imagine how this drink can be raw or healthy – let me watch you make it.'

720ml (1¼ pints) pecan nut milk (see p.33)
3 Medjool dates, pitted
1 ripe banana, peeled, chopped and frozen
3 tbsp manuka honey
2 tbsp lucuma powder
1 tsp vanilla powder or seeds from ½ vanilla pod

Nutty for Nog

I've never tried eggnog – the idea of it just doesn't jingle my bells. But it's clearly a popular drink and a seasonal favourite, so for my customers at Tanya's Café, I did a bit of ingredient comparison and substituted all the goods for plant-based versions. It turned out so good, we get asked for the Nut Nog many months after Christmas.

720ml (1¼ pints) hazelnut milk (see p.33)
2 bananas, peeled, chopped and frozen
4 tbsp Date Paste (see p.108) or
  3 Medjool dates, pitted
2 tsp mixed spice (I use a combination of
  coriander, cinnamon, clove, ginger and
  nutmeg)
1 tsp ground cinnamon
1 tsp ground turmeric
1 tsp vanilla extract

Work It Out

Perfect for a pre- or a post-workout regime, this drink has helped my clients to lose baby weight, run 100 miles and speed skate, and has for many become a favourite drink for training. For sustained energy and focus, and adrenal recovery, you need a balanced ratio between carbohydrates, protein and caffeine for staying power. This smoothie has been designed to deliver just the right balance in a delicious glassful, so you can focus on your training and push your body to the limits.

250ml (8½fl oz) coconut water
250ml (8½fl oz) hemp seed milk
  (see p.33)
80g (2¾oz) ripe pineapple, peeled,
  chopped and frozen
1 ripe banana, peeled, chopped and
  frozen
2 Medjool dates, pitted
2 tbsp desiccated coconut
1 tbsp sprouted buckwheat
2 tsp matcha powder
1 tsp maca powder
½ tsp spirulina powder

Blue Jump Start

Is it a milkshake? A breakfast? A dessert? Or is it a delicious, creamy glassful of antioxidants, Omega 3s, fibre and energy? You decide. Leave the oats to soak and soften in the milk overnight, then blend the lot in the morning, so energy can be redirected from digestion to something more fun.

400ml (14fl oz) walnut milk (see p.33)
150g (5½oz) blueberries
50g (1¾oz) gluten-free porridge oat
  flakes
1 banana, peeled, chopped and frozen
2 tbsp yacon syrup or agave nectar
1 tsp vanilla powder

Calcium Sunrise

Poppy seeds contain more calcium than any other source in either the plant or animal kingdom. Poppy seed milk contains twice the calcium of cow's milk and is much easier to digest. So give your bones a boost with this yummy drink.

600ml (1 pint) poppy seed milk (see p.33)
3 oranges, peeled, chopped and frozen
3 tbsp baobab powder
2 tbsp agave nectar
1 tsp spirulina powder
1 banana or ¼ avocado (optional)

Opening a Coconut

The coconut is a valuable source of nutrients and flavour in raw drinks and raw-food recipes. You can drink the water straight from the coconut, or use it in juices or smoothies. The flesh can be used to make many recipes, including smoothies.

Ask for a young coconut when you buy, such as the green one in the first picture on the opposite page – this is likely to come to you in shaved form, as shown opposite, between the young and mature coconuts. Use a sharp knife to shave off more of the husk at the top end.

Turn the coconut on its side, hold it firmly and, using a meat cleaver, give the shaved end a few taps at the top to locate soft areas. The shell is not solid, but is made up of tough round fragments that are joined by a soft, stretchy matter. As you tap the coconut, you will know you have found a good point at which to open it as the shell will suddenly feel softer, as if you're tapping a banana skin rather than a coconut. Whack the knife into the soft part you have located, then stand the coconut on its base and twist the knife to pop up the loosened top and open the coconut.

Pour out the water and strain it to remove sharp shell fragments. Drink it now or keep it refrigerated for up to 7 days. Look out for discoloured, cloudy or smelly water and give it a taste-test before using it in recipes.

Scrape out the flesh with a metal spoon or a rubber spatula. Place in filtered water and scrape off any shell shards with your fingers. Refrigerate in an airtight container for up to 4 days or freeze for up to 2 months.

Coconuts & Coconut Products

The coconut palm has the largest seed and flower cluster within the plant kingdom. The plant has so many uses, it has made tropical living sustainable for centuries. I hear much confusion about coconut types – there is just one. Green coconuts are young, whereas brown coconuts are mature.

Fresh coconuts When a coconut falls from the tree or is harvested at eight months of maturity, it is referred to as a young green coconut and is full of electrolyte-rich water. The flesh is soft, transparent and jelly-like. At this stage of development, both the water and flesh are at their peak in terms of nutrition. The coconut is then often shaved at its place of origin to what we recognise as a white cone-head coconut. This is to make it less heavy and less bulky to transport. As it matures away from the tree, the water becomes sweeter and the flesh more dense. Eventually, the thick fibrous husk on unshaved coconuts dries, shrinks and turns brown. The flesh grows and becomes thicker and oilier, while the water starts to evaporate into sweet, syrupy residue. This coconut is often seen in supermarkets.

Coconut products Coconut milk and virgin oil are derived from the thick flesh in a matured coconut. Coconut flour is what remains after the oil is taken. Coconut butter is produced by drying the flesh, then grinding it to a spread. Dried or dehydrated grated flesh is sold as shredded coconut and coconut flakes. Coconut syrup and sugar are crystallised coconut tree sap.

From top: Mexican Hot Chocolate, Matcha love

Hot Drinks

EACH SERVES 2

There's no reason why you can't enjoy hot drinks on a raw-food diet or detox routine because, as long as you don't brew the ingredients over a stove, you won't be cooking them. To make the first three recipes, simply blend the ingredients in a blender on a high speed setting, pour and enjoy.

Matcha Love

Matcha has 100 times the antioxidants found in regular green tea. Because it comes in powdered form, you ingest the leaf, taking in all the beneficial chlorophyll. And it is delicious!

600ml (1 pint) hot water
4 Medjool dates, pitted, or 10 pitted
  dates, soaked for 4–6 hours
2 heaped tbsp coconut butter
1 tsp matcha powder

Mushroom Latte

This is the most popular hot drink at Tanya's Café. I like to vary my medicinal mushrooms for this latte, alternating between cordyceps for energy, reishi for relaxation and chaga for immunity.

600ml (1 pint) hot water
4 Medjool dates, pitted, or 10 pitted
  dates, soaked for 4–6 hours
2 heaped tbsp Almond Butter (see p.109)
2 tsp cordyceps, reishi, chaga or the
  medicinal mushroom of your choice

Mexican Hot Chocolate

Cayenne pepper stimulates the circulatory system, aids digestion and helps to regulate blood sugar. Just imagine what magic can happen when you marry it with antioxidant- and magnesium-rich cacao! This hot chocolate is just as healthy as it is tasty.

600ml (1 pint) hot water
4 Medjool dates, pitted, or 10 pitted
  dates, soaked for 4–6 hours
2 heaped tbsp Almond Butter (see p.109)
2 tbsp raw cacao powder
1 tbsp manuka honey or agave nectar
1 tsp ground cinnamon
½ tsp cayenne pepper
¼ avocado (optional)

Healing Tea

Virtually any herbs or edible flowers and fruits can be made into a comforting, nutritious cuppa – just pour over some hot water. Below I list suitable fruits, flowers, herbs and grasses. Dehydrate any of these at 48°C for 20–40 hours, then add to hot water. Mix and match to craft blends stamped with your zest and personality.

Ideas for herbs and grasses:
Lemongrass, mint, nettle, catnip, fennel, passion flower leaf, blackberry leaf, hibiscus, cleavers, valerian, dandelion, basil, sage, rosemary, Pau D'arco leaf and bark.

Ideas for flowers:
Jasmine, heather, bee balm, chamomile, rose petals, lavender, echinacea, hibiscus, lilac, calendula, amaranth, carnation, elderflower, safflower.

Ideas for fruits:
Peach, apple, apricot, rosehip, orange peel, lemon peel, chicory root, ginger root, hawthorn, strawberry, goji berry, all berries.

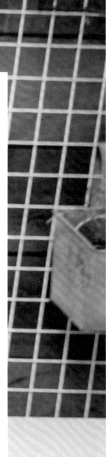

CHAPTER 2

Breakfasts

Breakfast isn't known as the most important meal of the day for no reason – it's vital to get it right, as you are breaking a fast after sleeping. While your body is still waking up and slowly turning on its digestive system, it's always a good idea to support it with something easy to process and assimilate for an energising boost. Don't be surprised if these delicious enzyme-rich recipes start replacing your 3 o'clock snacks, too.

Green Warming Oat Porridge

— SERVES 1

This porridge recipe came about by chance and now I'm obsessed. One day I made a jug of delicious green juice to sip while developing recipes, but as I reached for a loosely tied bag of oats, they tumbled into the juice. I couldn't bring myself to bin such quality organic ingredients, so decided to taste the concoction. It was so yummy that this dish is now a morning staple.

240ml (8¼ fl oz) green juice (try my
 favourite on p.24, or buy ready-made
 juice from an organic café)
100g (3oz) gluten-free porridge oat
 flakes

Optional toppings:
fresh or dried fruit, desiccated coconut,
 goji berries, bee pollen

If you're making the green juice from scratch, prepare it with fruits and veggies that are kept out of the refrigerator for 24 hours beforehand – they will be a good temperature for a 'warming' porridge.

Once you have made your juice, mix it with the oat flakes in a bowl and set aside for 10–20 minutes to allow the oats to soak up the liquids and soften into a porridge. Better yet, mix it the night before and leave it to soak at room temperature overnight, for a ready breakfast to wake up to.

Enjoy topped with fresh or dried fruit, or any topping of your choice.

Acai Bowl

— SERVES 1

You can make Acai Bowl using only frozen fruits for a sorbet-type breakfast, and add almond butter for a creamier version. I prefer the fruit-only variety, as this way, the meal is more digestible – it follows the alkalising food-combining principles.

80g (2¾oz) strawberries
50g (1¾oz) blueberries
1 Medjool date, pitted
1 tsp vanilla extract
100g (3oz) frozen unsweetened acai
 berry pulp
½ ripe banana, chopped and frozen

Optional toppings:
Crunchy Granola Clusters (see p.46),
 coconut flakes, bee pollen, fresh fruit

Blend the fresh berries, the date and the vanilla to a paste in a blender.

Run the unopened packet of acai pulp under cold running water for about 30 seconds to defrost it, then cut the pulp in half and pop it into the blender jug with the blended ingredients. Add the frozen banana and, using the tamper, blend on a high speed setting.

Transfer the mixture to a bowl and enjoy on its own or sprinkled with granola or anything else delicious and breakfasty.

Clockwise from top: Apple Cinnamon Chia Porridge (see p.45), Acai Bowl, Green Warming Oat Porridge

Coconut Chia Porridge

Chia Porridges

I love everything about chia seeds – how nutritious they are, their versatility and, also, I love the name. I use them in so many of my recipes – from sweet jellies and spreads to savoury crackers and breads – but there's something extra magical about starting the day with a heartening bowl of chia porridge. Plus, anything that makes you fantasise about high-fiving with the Aztec warriors first thing in the morning has got to be good for you.

Apple Cinnamon Chia

– *SERVES 2*

480ml (17fl oz) almond milk (see p.33)
2 golden eating apples, peeled and cored
2 Medjool dates, pitted
2 tsp ground cinnamon
45g (1¾oz) chia seeds

Optional toppings:
bee pollen, raw honey, chopped tangy
  fruit, fresh berries

Coconut Chia

– *SERVES 2*

720ml (1¼ pints) almond milk (see p.33),
  or coconut milk (see p.36) for a nut-free
  version
3 tbsp maple syrup
2 tbsp coconut butter
1 tbsp vanilla extract
pinch of Himalayan salt
90g (3oz) chia seeds

Optional toppings:
coconut flakes, goji berries, chopped
  creamy fruit, cacao nibs

Put all the ingredients, except the chia seeds and optional toppings, into a blender and blend together.

Transfer to a jug, stir in the chia seeds and stir rapidly for 1 minute so the seeds don't clump up as they begin to form a gel. Now leave to set for 10 minutes, stirring the mixture every couple of minutes. (Alternatively, leave the mixture in your blender, add the chia seeds and pulse on the lowest speed setting to stir the porridge, but watch the seeds so they don't become too ground up, or you'll be left with a paste, not a porridge.)

Transfer the mixture to bowls, sprinkle with extras and enjoy right away or store in the refrigerator for a maximum of 4 days.

Crunchy Granola Clusters

— SERVES 8

If you aren't very good with nuts, you'll find that, after soaking them and rinsing away the enzyme inhibitors, they become lighter and much easier on your digestion. Adding the buckwheat, a gluten-free powerhouse of protein, and a delicious sticky mix, makes this raw granola simply the best.

For the crunchy mix:
180g (6¼oz) sprouted buckwheat
60g (2oz) sunflower seeds, soaked for
  4–6 hours
75g (2¾oz) hazelnuts, soaked for
  6–8 hours
75g (2¾oz) almonds, soaked for 6–8 hours
45g (1¾oz) desiccated coconut

For the sticky mix:
300g (10½oz) pitted dates, soaked for
  4–6 hours, reserving the soaking liquid
2 tbsp ground cinnamon
1 tbsp mixed spice
1 tsp Himalayan salt
algarroba, carob, cacao or lucuma
  powders, to taste (optional)

To sprout the buckwheat, soak the dry groats in water for 5 hours, then rinse thoroughly. Continue to rinse until the water is no longer gooey – I usually rinse them 4 times. Leave the buckwheat out on a flat tray for 24 hours, rinsing twice more over that period of time.

Roughly chop the remaining crunchy mix ingredients, or use the pulse setting on a food processor to break them up into uneven chunks.

Process or blend all the sticky mix ingredients to a smooth consistency, adding the sweet water in which the dates were soaked, if needed, to obtain a creamy texture.

Combine both mixes in a large bowl, then spread the mixture on 2–3 Teflex sheets (see p.19). Dehydrate at 48°C for 15 hours, then transfer onto mesh sheets and dehydrate for 15–20 hours until fully dry and crunchy.

Break up the granola into cluster chunks and store in an airtight container. Serve with your favourite nut milk and berries or, if you are like me, snack away on the clusters.

Goji Jam

— FILLS A 400ML (14FL OZ) JAR

Goji berries are high in antioxidants, fibre, iron and protein, low in calories and are fat free, and because they raise blood sugar slowly, this tasty jam won't give you a sugar crash after breakfast.

150g (5½oz) frozen strawberries, defrosted
100g (3oz) frozen raspberries, defrosted
2 tbsp raw honey or agave nectar
30g (1¼oz) goji berries, soaked in
  120ml (4fl oz) water for 2–4 hours
2 tbsp chia seeds

Process the strawberries, raspberries and honey in a food processor with an S-blade.

Add the soaked goji berries and the chia seeds, then pulse a couple of times until the berries are slightly broken down but still chunky.

Transfer the textured jam to a sterilised lidded jar and store in the refrigerator for up to 5 days.

Clockwise from top: Crunchy Granola Clusters, Coconut Yogurt (see p.53), Goji Jam

Aubergine Bacon

Aubergine Bacon

— SERVES 2-3

Perhaps 'bacon' isn't the best word here. Or maybe it is. Mmmnn... bacon... If, like me, you gave up meat but have sweet memories of bacon, these tempting strips will make everything better. You're welcome.

2 aubergines
80ml (3fl oz) apple cider vinegar
4 tbsp tamari
3 tbsp raw liquid honey or maple syrup
2 tsp sweet smoked paprika
banana and maple syrup, to serve
  (optional)

Snap off the aubergine caps. Slice the fruit lengthwise on a mandoline set no thinner than 5mm (¼in). Use a damp tea towel to hold the aubergine when slicing to keep your fingers safe.

Mix the remaining ingredients in a bowl. Dip the aubergine strips in one at a time to coat. Marinate for 1 hour.

Place the strips side-by-side on a Teflex sheet and dehydrate at 45°C for 4 hours. Transfer onto mesh trays, coat with any remaining marinade and dehydrate for another 4 hours.

Enjoy the chewy strips alone or with banana slices and maple syrup. Store in an airtight box for up to 1 week.

Muesli Bread

—SERVES 6-10

This gluten-free raw bread is sure to banish any bread cravings. Delicious on its own, it's especially tasty spread with Almond Butter (see p.109) and Goji Jam (see p.46) or Coconut Yogurt (see p.53).

150g (5½oz) almonds, soaked for 6–8 hours
120g (4¼oz) sunflower seeds, soaked for
  4–6 hours
135g (4¾oz) pumpkin seeds, soaked
  for 4–6 hours
1 courgette, peeled
2 eating apples, peeled and cored
1 ripe pineapple, peeled and cored
50g (1¾oz) gluten-free porridge oat flakes
50g (1¾oz) ground flaxseeds
3 tbsp extra virgin olive oil
2 tsp ground cinnamon
1 tsp vanilla powder
½ tsp Himalayan salt

Combine the nuts and seeds in a food processor with an S-blade until ground. Use a spatula to clean the side of the bowl, returning the mix to the blades.

Chop the courgette and fruits, then add them to the food processor with the remaining ingredients. Process everything into a wet, grainy dough.

Divide the mixture in half and spread each half to a thickness of 1cm (½in)

over Teflex sheets. Dehydrate at 48°C for 10 hours. Turn out onto mesh trays, peel off the Teflex sheets and return to the dehydrator for another 10 hours. The bread will be soft, but if you are after a more dense, chewy version, leave it in the dehydrator for a further 5 hours.

Cut into any desired shape. Store in an airtight container for up to 2 weeks.

Spinach & Cashew-Cheddar Quiche

— SERVES 6

A little forward planning will make a special occasion all the more memorable with this delicious quiche. It keeps well in the fridge for up to two weeks, so you can enjoy any leftovers with a juicy salad at any time of day.

For the base:

130g (4½oz) cashew nuts, soaked for
  4–6 hours
150g (5½oz) almonds, soaked for
  6–8 hours
100g (3oz) ground flaxseed
1 white onion
2 garlic cloves, minced
3 tbsp extra virgin olive oil, plus extra for
  oiling
1 tbsp nutritional yeast
1 tbsp lemon juice
½ tsp Himalayan salt

For the 'Cheddar' filling:

100g (3oz) pine nuts
100g (3oz) macadamia nuts
120ml (4fl oz) water
80ml (3fl oz) extra virgin olive oil
8 sundried tomato halves, soaked if too
  dry
juice of 1 lemon
2 tbsp liquid aminos
2 garlic cloves
1 tsp sweet smoked paprika

For the spinach:

60g (2oz) spinach leaves

To garnish (optional):

basil leaves and/or micro leaves

Prepare 6 mini (10cm/4in) loose-bottomed tartlet tins by oiling all the inside surfaces.

Process all the base ingredients in a food processor with an S-blade. Divide the mixture evenly between the prepared tins. Using your fingers, press the dough into the bottom and up the side of each pan to create a crust.

Transfer the tins to the dehydrator and dehydrate for 10 hours at 48°C. Remove all casings, including the bottoms, and return the crusts to the dehydrator for another 10 hours on mesh trays.

Prepare the filling by blending all the ingredients in a blender until creamy. Transfer to a large bowl.

Roughly chop the spinach and stir it into the filling mixture.

Divide the filling into 6 equal portions and scoop 1 portion into each of the shaped crusts. Smooth the tops slightly. Return the filled crusts to the dehydrator for another 6–8 hours.

TANYA'S
TOP TIP

To serve the quiche warm, pop it back into the dehydrator for 2 hours before serving.

From top: Coconut Yogurt, Goji Jam (see p.46), Fruit Crêpes

Fruit Crêpes

– SERVES 2

Long before I discovered dehydrators and that gluten is 'glu-ten' (i.e. 'glue-times-ten') in your gut, I loved pancakes. Crêpes were even more special. At the time I believed the word was pronounced as 'creepies', which was entertaining in my then-Russian accent. This raw version is just as moreish.

For the crêpes:
3 ripe bananas, peeled and chopped
2 tbsp ground flaxseeds
½ tsp vanilla powder
pinch of Himalayan salt

For the filling:
your favourite fruit salad
Goji Jam (see p.46)
Coconut Yogurt (see below)
maple syrup

Blend all the crêpe ingredients to a cream in a blender. Pour the mixture onto 2 Teflex sheets in 4 mounds. Use a spatula to smooth them out into circles that are no less than 5mm (¼in) in thickness.

Dehydrate at 48°C for 4 hours, or until the crêpes are dry to the touch. Take care not to mess up the surfaces by touching them too early. Think of it as you would when painting your nails – no touching the nail polish until you are sure it is dry!

Carefully peel off the crêpes and transfer to a mesh sheet. Dehydrate for a further 1–3 hours until dry, yet pliable without cracking when bent. (If you find the crêpes are over-dry and start to crack, run a wet brush over the dry edges.)

Fill with your favourite fruit salad or goji jam and coconut yogurt and roll into tubes or fold in half, then drizzle with maple syrup to serve.

Coconut Yogurt

– FILLS A 400ML (14FL OZ) JAR

I still remember my first pot of yogurt – a strawberry-flavoured creamy delight. I'm now conscious of what goes into those little pots and prefer to make my own yogurt, stirred with Goji Jam (see p.46), strawberries, muesli and raw honey, which takes me back to being the happiest nine-year-old in the world.

2 capsules dairy-free probiotic
300g (10½oz) young coconut flesh
120ml (4fl oz) coconut water
juice of 1 lime

Open the probiotic capsules and tip out the contents into a blender jug. Add the remaining ingredients and blend until creamy. Pour into a glass jar, cover with a damp cheesecloth and leave to sit at room temperature for 10–15 hours.

Stir the mixture, secure the jar with a lid and transfer to the refrigerator. Store for up to 10 days.

CHAPTER 3

Soups & Salads

Of all the sections in this book, this is the one
that always makes me think of family. I was
brought up on soups and there was no shortage
of imagination in Mum when it came to creating
soups that the whole family would love. As
my parents discovered raw food, mastering
the tastiest soup was first on their agenda. It is
equally key to get the balance right with salads
if you want them to provide you with a proper
meal that both hydrates and satisfies.

Cream of Shiitake Mushroom Soup

— SERVES 3

This recipe will always remind me of Latvia. Not long ago, when my friend's baby girl was born, I went to see them both in Riga, the place of my dad's ex-military base, and we went mushroom foraging, which inspired the recipe. It is comforting, satisfying and nourishing, just like the quality time spent with family.

150g (5½oz) shiitake mushrooms
720ml (1¼ pints) almond milk (see p.33)
3 celery sticks, chopped
½ red onion, chopped
3 garlic cloves
juice of 1 lemon
2 tbsp liquid aminos

Reserve a couple of mushrooms for garnish, if you like, and put the rest, along with the other ingredients, in a blender. Blend on a high speed setting until the soup begins to warm up.

Serve straight after blending or add boiling water to the soup to warm it up at a later stage.

TANYA'S TOP TIP

A little bread or some croûtons liven up any soup. There is something about this particular dish that just calls for crunchy Croûtons (see p.109) – it's as if the two were meant to be.

Alkaline Soup

— SERVES 3

What do you do for fun? I face-paint, balloon-sculpt, sprout-whisper and test my pH levels. I never said I wasn't weird, but testing your pH levels before and after a meal to see how the meal has affected your acid-alkaline balance is rather fun. You can buy litmus paper from a pharmacy and try it for yourself. This soup will tip your balance in the alkaline direction. It always does for me.

480ml (17fl oz) water
120g (4¼oz) fresh peas
80g (2¾oz) Soured Cream made with
  cashew nuts (see p.106)
juice of 2 limes
1 celery stick, chopped
½ avocado
1 garlic clove

3 tbsp Date Paste (see p.108) or
  3 Medjool dates, pitted
small handful of parsley
1 tsp thyme leaves
Himalayan salt and ground black pepper,
  to taste
peas, cracked pepper and parsley, to
  garnish (optional)

Blend all the ingredients, except the garnish, in a blender on a high speed setting until creamy. Check the seasoning, adjust if needed and blend again. Garnish and serve. The soup is delicious served chilled. To warm it up, add a pinch of cayenne pepper and boiling water just before serving.

Cream of Shiitake Mushroom Soup with crunchy Croûtons (see p.109)

From left: Pumpkin Soup, Russian Borshch

Pumpkin Soup

— SERVES 3

Pumpkins are full of fibre, beta-carotene, Vitamic C, potassium, iron, calcium, copper, phosphorous and zinc, which promote healthy skin and boost immunity. Vitamin C slows down ageing and protects the body from disease and pollution. One serving of raw pumpkin provides half the recommended daily dose of vitamin C. Mother Nature doesn't give us pumpkins in flu season for no reason.

450g (1lb) butternut squash or pumpkin, peeled and chopped
3 tomatoes, chopped
1 golden eating apple, chopped
240ml (8¼fl oz) seed milk (see p.33)
juice of 1 lemon
2 tbsp raw tahini
1cm (½in) root ginger
½ red chilli, deseeded if you like it mild

2 garlic cloves
1 tbsp dried thyme
1 tsp ground turmeric
½ tsp Himalayan salt
pinch of ground black pepper
Soured Cream made with cashew nuts (see p.106), small cubes of pumpkin, pumpkin seeds and parsley, to garnish (optional)

Blend the ingredients, except the garnishes, using a tamper or by pulsing. The soup will be warming from the chilli, but if you like the temperature to be warm, too, blend for 4 minutes on a high speed setting or add some hot water while blending – added this late, the hot water won't have a chance to cripple the veggies. Garnish, then serve.

Russian Borshch

— SERVES 2

In Russia, lunch was the biggest meal of the day and it always seemed to be soup – a fussy kid's worst nightmare, especially when it was borshch! But now, I'm in love with the colours, flavours and textures of this motherland classic and obsessed with making it even better raw (get it? BetterRaw.com).

For the liquids:
1 beetroot, peeled and chopped
1 red pepper, deseeded and chopped
1 celery stick, chopped
2.5cm (1in) root ginger
2–3 garlic cloves
240ml (8¼fl oz) orange juice (juice of 2–3 oranges)
4 tbsp extra virgin olive oil

2 tbsp apple cider vinegar
1 tsp chilli powder
1 tsp ground coriander
1 tsp Himalayan salt
For the solids:
Sauerkraut (see p.64) or carrot, beetroot and cabbage, to taste,
herbs
walnut pieces

Combine the liquid ingredients in a blender, blending and pulsing for 3-4 minutes until smooth.

Scoop as much sauerkraut as you want to eat into each soup bowl, pour over the soup, sprinkle with herbs and walnuts, then serve. Or thinly slice peeled carrots, beetroot and cabbage to use instead of the sauerkraut.

Gazpacho

— SERVES 3

This refreshing and energising gazpacho has endless health benefits in the combination of veggies used and the inclusion of apple cider vinegar, a fermented product that improves digestion and intestinal health. To add to the benefits, we are leaving the soup to ferment further in the refrigerator.

For the liquids:
5 large ripe tomatoes
240ml (8¼fl oz) water
35g (1¼oz) basil
2 garlic cloves
3 tbsp lemon juice
2 tbsp apple cider vinegar
2 tbsp raw honey or 2 Medjool dates, pitted
2 tbsp extra virgin olive oil
½ tsp Himalayan salt

For the solids:
1 red pepper, deseeded
⅓ large cucumber
2 celery sticks
150g (5½oz) pineapple, peeled and cored
1 avocado
herbs of your choice, to taste

Blend the liquids ingredients together in a blender until smooth.

Chop all the solids ingredients into small cubes, put them in a bowl and stir them together to mix up the colours. Scoop a helping of this mixture into each of 3 soup bowls, reserving some for garnish, and pour the liquid part on top. Sprinkle with the reserved cubed veggies to serve.

Elena's Yellow Soup

— SERVES 4

Everyone on my retreats knows that my mum is the queen of soups. Despite Mum's best efforts to name this recipe Sage Soup, just the mention of 'Elena's Yellow Soup' is enough to get us salivating.

For the liquids:
480ml (17fl oz) water
300g (10½oz) celery sticks, chopped
70g (2½oz) pitted dates, soaked for 4-6 hours
juice of 1 lime
1 tbsp extra virgin olive oil
1 tbsp dried sage, soaked in 3 tbsp hot water for 1 hour
2 tsp ground turmeric
1 tsp Himalayan salt
½ tsp garlic powder
½ tsp ground ginger

For the solids:
1 eating apple, peeled
100g (3oz) sauerkraut and/or 1 carrot, peeled
¼ red or yellow pepper, deseeded
100g (3oz) cucumber
2 avocados
fresh herbs, to taste
Soured Cream (see p.106), to taste (optional)

Blend the 'liquids' ingredients together in a blender until smooth.

Grate the apple and the carrot, if you're using the carrot. Cube the pepper, cucumber and avocados. Put the prepared vegetables in a bowl, pour over the soup and stir. To serve, divide the soup amongst 4 bowls, sprinkle with herbs and top with the cashew soured cream.

Gazpacho

Hearty Kale Salad

— SERVES 2

This is the raw food dish I make most often. To me it ticks all the boxes. It's a salad, yet is filling; it's detoxifying, yet is nourishing; it's a powerhouse of magnesium, calcium and amino acids, yet it tastes too good to tell. Make the base salad and serve as a side or add your favourite veggies for a full meal.

1 large carrot, peeled
1 sweet potato, peeled
1 super-ripe avocado
70g (2½oz) pitted olives
4 sundried tomato halves

For the base salad:
200g (7oz) kale
2 tbsp extra virgin olive oil
2 tbsp lemon juice
2 tbsp orange juice
¼ tsp Himalayan salt

To prepare the base salad, wash the kale, as it's likely to be covered in dirt and sand – the good stuff when organic, but not so good on the teeth. Cut off the tough stalks and chop the leaves into 2.5cm (½in) chunks. Put the chopped leaves in a bowl, drizzle over the remaining base salad ingredients and massage them into the leaves until they soften and change colour to a more vivid green.

Grate the carrot and raw sweet potato, or spiralise them. Slice, chop or cut the remaining ingredients to your liking, toss with the kale salad and serve.

TANYA'S
TOP TIP

The salt in the base salad will help to break down the cell walls of the firm kale leaves, making them easier to digest..

Comforting Mushroom Salad

— SERVES 2

While most mushrooms are available all year round, shiitake are at their peak in autumn and winter. They are dense, meaty and filling, so when I'm missing a hearty meal, this one hits the spot. They also contain iron, protein, fibre, vitamin C and selenium, making them an ideal immunity booster.

150g (5½oz) cavolo nero
2 carrots, peeled
2 tomatoes
1 avocado

For the mushroom jus:
150g (5½oz) shiitake mushrooms
2 tbsp liquid aminos

2 tbsp extra virgin olive oil
juice of ½ lemon
1 tbsp white miso paste

To make the jus, slice the mushrooms into equal chunks. Mix with the other jus ingredients in a bowl. Marinate for 1 hour. Cut off the cavolo nero stalks and roughly chop the leaves. Grate the carrots. Slice the tomatoes and avocado. Put the prepared veggies in a large bowl, pour in the jus and toss.

Sauerkraut

— MAKES 1.3KG (2LB 13OZ)

I was inspired to make this recipe when I visited Poland, where sauerkraut was on every menu. And no wonder – it's amazing. I always feel so good after eating it. While the cabbage ferments, it predigests, so it's a good digestion aid to any meal. The probiotics are essential for a happy gut, too.

1kg (2lb 4oz) cabbage
200–300g (7–10½oz) carrots, peeled
25g (1oz) Himalayan salt
1 tbsp raw honey
1 tsp probiotic powder (approximately 4 capsules)
10 whole black peppercorns
pinch of caraway seeds

Remove and reserve the outer cabbage leaves. Thinly slice the cabbage. Grate the carrots. Put the prepared veggies in a bowl with the other ingredients and massage well, applying force.

Line the base of a large saucepan with the reserved cabbage leaves. Transfer the cabbage-and-carrot mixture to the cabbage-lined pot and squash it down with your fist. Position a plate directly on top of the cabbage, ensuring it covers the entire mixture, then place a weight on top (I use a jug filled with water, or a coconut, when I have one).

Every day for 5 days, uncover the mixture twice a day and poke holes into it to allow trapped air to escape, then replace the plate and weight. After 5 days, transfer to sealable glass jars and keep refrigerated.

Pineapple Salsa

— SERVES 6 AS A SIDE DISH

I was never that big on salsa. And then I discovered raw foods. I learned that salsa gets tastier with each day, which is a massive bonus when following a diet that, supposedly, has 'too much preparation involved' and in which 'nothing keeps'. I love these myths – almost as much as I love salsa.

200g (7oz) ripe pineapple
½ small onion, peeled
3 tomatoes
30g (1¼oz) parsley, finely chopped
juice of 2 limes
2 tbsp extra virgin olive oil
1 tsp ground cumin
pinch of Himalayan salt

Peel off the pineapple skin. Remove the core. Chop the pineapple, onion and tomatoes into tiny equal cubes. Put the cubed veggies in a bowl, add the remaining ingredients and toss well. Marinate, refrigerated, for at least 3 hours. The flavour will improve over time. Keep refrigerated for up to 5 days.

TANYA'S
TOP TIP

The key to a winning salsa is to ensure all the chopped ingredients are small and uniformly cubed.

Sauerkraut

The Best Kale Kelp Salad Ever

The Best Kale Kelp Salad Ever

— SERVES 2

I've seen both adults and kids go crazy for this salad and I think I know why... Toasted sesame seeds are a naughty exception to the raw rule here. My theory goes like this – their moreish flavour makes you consume so much more of this highly nutritious salad than you would without them!

340g (11¾oz) kelp noodles
1 quantity kale base salad (see p.63)
chopped ripe avocado, sesame seeds and
  olives, to garnish (optional)

For the dressing:
3 tbsp sesame seeds, toasted
3 tbsp liquid aminos or tamari
3 tbsp lime juice

3 tbsp extra virgin olive oil
2 tbsp nutritional yeast
2 garlic cloves
7 pitted dates, soaked for 4–6 hours
1 tbsp raw honey
120ml (4fl oz) water

Blend the dressing ingredients in a blender until creamy.

Place the noodles in a bowl. Pour in the dressing and massage it into them. Leave to stand for 10–30 minutes. Toss with the kale, sprinkle with the optional ingredients and serve.

Root Veggie Satay Noodles

— SERVES 2

When I first tasted satay noodles, I never wanted anything else again, so I avoided reading the labels for fear of being put off. When I finally succumbed, I wasn't surprised to spot all the nasties in there, but I was determined to satisfy my satay obsession. This healthy version won't disappoint!

2 carrots, peeled
1 sweet potato, peeled
100g (3oz) Jerusalem artichokes,
  scrubbed
handful of bean sprouts
handful of pine nuts or hemp seeds
  (optional)

For the sauce:
180ml (6fl oz) nut or seed milk (see p.33)
2 tbsp tamari
2 tbsp toasted sesame oil
2 tbsp desiccated coconut

1 tbsp almond butter
6 pitted dates, soaked for 4–6 hours
juice of ½ lime
2.5cm (1in) root ginger
1 tbsp yacon syrup, maple syrup or
  agave nectar
½ chilli or ¼ tsp cayenne pepper
1 garlic clove

Blend the sauce ingredients in a blender until smooth.

Using a spiraliser, a potato peeler or even a grater, create noodle shapes with the carrots, sweet potato and Jerusalem artichokes. Put the noodles in a bowl, add the remaining salad ingredients and toss to mix. Pour the sauce over the top and give the mixture a good stir. Keep at room temperature until ready to serve.

Tomato & Avocado Salad

— SERVES 4

When I work a shift at the café, my kitchen team don't even ask what I'd like for a staff meal any more – this baby's already waiting for me. If only there were an alternative word for 'obsessed' that has a healthy implication, I'd use it to describe my love for a good ol' tomato and avocado salad!

4 ripe avocados
8 vine tomatoes
3 handfuls of baby salad leaves

For the balsamic vinaigrette:
180ml (6fl oz) extra virgin olive oil
4 tbsp balsamic vinegar
3 tbsp lemon juice
½ tsp ground pepper
½ tsp Himalayan salt

Slice the avocado lengthwise and along the width with the tip of a knife. Gently slide a spoon between the skin and flesh to scoop out the flesh. Chop the tomatoes into smallish cubes.

Put all the vinaigrette ingredients into a sealable jar, seal shut and shake the jar to combine the ingredients.

To serve, toss the chopped tomatoes with the vinaigrette and serve over a bed of baby salad leaves. Alternatively, toss the tomatoes, avocados and baby salad leaves together and allow your guests to pour their desired quantity of dressing on top.

Caesar Salad

— SERVES 3

Prior to the rawsome days, I would often order a Caesar salad when eating out. When researching acid-alkaline balance, I learned that parmesan, bacon and anchovies are all highly acidic. So I developed a plant-based alternative as a healthy homage to the well-loved classic.

2 heads of romaine lettuce
3 celery sticks
½ quantity Caramelised Onions (see p.110), Coconut Jerky (see p.140) or Crunchy Croûtons (see p.109), to garnish

For the Caesar dressing:
45g (1¾oz) cashew nuts, soaked for 4–6 hours
30g (1¼oz) sunflower seeds, soaked for 4–6 hours

50g (1¾oz) pine nuts
4 tbsp lemon juice
3 Medjool dates, pitted
2 tbsp tamari
1 tbsp raw tahini
2 tsp Dijon mustard
1–2 garlic cloves
1 tbsp white miso paste
½ tsp dried dill
ground black pepper, to taste
120ml (4fl oz) water

Blend the dressing ingredients in a high-powered blender. If the sauce is too thick, add a little more water, but ensure you don't make the dressing too runny.

Chop the romaine into 2.5cm (1in) chunks and the celery into 1cm (½in) nuggets. Put the prepared veggies in a bowl with the dressing, toss well, garnish and serve immediately.

From top: Tomato & Avocado Salad, Caesar Salad

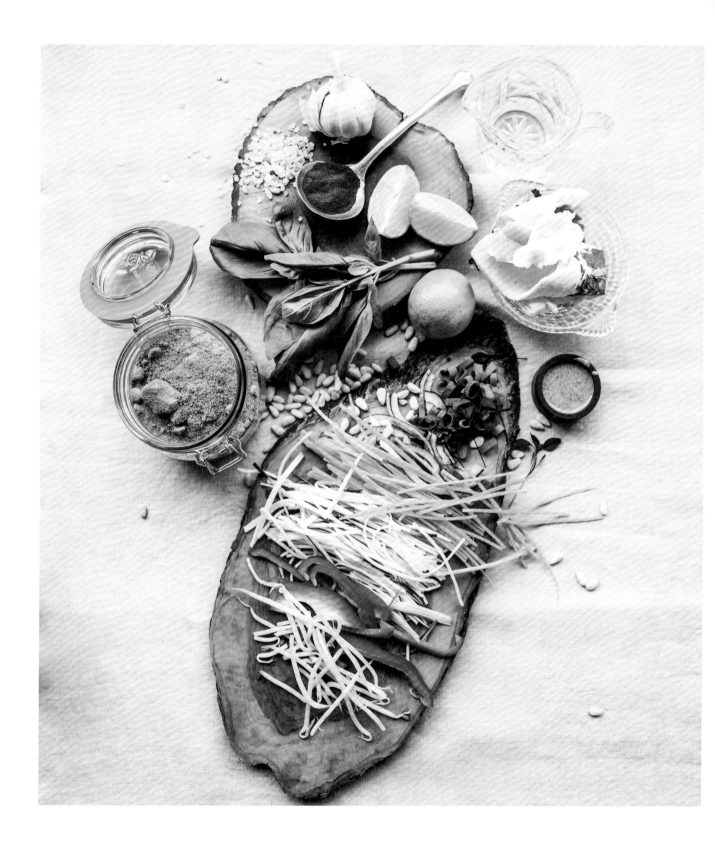

Pad Thai

— SERVES 5

Young green coconuts (as opposed to matured brown-shell coconuts) have tremendous antiviral properties due to their high level of strengthening medium-chain fatty acids and electrolyte-rich water content. The jelly meat is particularly good for cleansing the urinary tract, bladder and kidneys, and also for building muscle and tissue. It's delicious even on its own, but if you were to make the best possible recipe to use it in, this Pad Thai is it!

3 courgettes

3 carrots

2 red peppers

1 red onion

60g (2oz) bean sprouts

green onions, pine nuts and black sesame
  seeds, to garnish

For the sauce:

250g (9oz) coconut meat

240ml (8¼fl oz) water

20g (¾oz) basil

40g (1½oz) coconut palm sugar

3 garlic cloves

zest and juice of 2 limes

1 tbsp Almond Butter (see p.109)

2 tsp paprika

2 tsp Himalayan salt

½–1 tsp cayenne pepper (optional)

Put all the sauce ingredients into a blender, adding the cayenne pepper if you prefer a hotter spice mixture, and blend to a cream.

Spiralise or julienne the courgettes and carrots. Thinly slice both the peppers and onion into long strips. Put the prepared vegetables in a bowl with the bean sprouts and toss to combine the ingredients. Pour the dressing over the sauce and mix everything together thoroughly.

Distribute the Pad Thai equally among 5 serving plates using tongs or salad servers. Sprinkle over your desired quantity of garnishes and serve immediately.

TANYA'S
TOP TIP

It is not always easy to get hold of fresh young coconut flesh, so when it is available, buy plenty and make extra Pad Thai sauce to freeze. It will keep for up to 4 months. Simply defrost, blend and serve immediately.

Chinese Spice Salad

— SERVES 2–3

I love how some recipes just happen and come together simply from all the ingredients I have left in my refrigerator. I especially love how those ingredients usually happen to be the ones I like best and therefore purchase most often, so I am highly likely to find them whenever I need to make this super quick, satisfying and visually striking salad.

1 small cauliflower, finely chopped
6 asparagus stems, cut into small dice
3 celery sticks, cut into small dice
1 conference pear, cut into small dice
25g (1oz) chives, chopped
2 heads of red chicory (optional)

For the cream:
4 tbsp tamari
3 tbsp raw tahini
2 tbsp raw honey
1 tbsp grated root ginger
2 tbsp warm water
chilli flakes, to taste (optional)

Stir together the cream ingredients in a bowl, adding the chilli flakes if you prefer a bit of a punch.

Put the cauliflower, asparagus, celery, pear and chives in a large bowl and toss together. If you're using the red chicory, assemble the leaves on a plate, dish the salad mix on top and drizzle with the creamy dressing. If you're not using chicory leaves, dish the mixed salad in generous uneven lines right across the serving plates and drizzle with the cream, ensuring some of the cream lands on the plates, too.

The creamy dressing in this recipe also makes a delicious dip or spread. It keeps well – refrigerate it for up to 4 weeks, or it will be fine at room temperature for up to 5 days, so you can take it travelling with you!

From left: Sweet & Tangy Cabbage Salad, Cucumber & Sea

Sweet & Tangy Cabbage Salad

— SERVES 4

This salad is kinda perfect. It's crunchy, sweet, tangy, salty, creamy and pink! What more could a girl (or a stylish guy) want? I like to leave this salad at room temperature for four to six hours after preparation, so the cabbage can really soak up the flavours, but it's delicious served straightaway, too.

1 small red cabbage
100g (3oz) mixed bean sprouts
250g (9oz) baby spinach

For the dressing:
110g (4oz) frozen raspberries, defrosted
juice of ½ lemon
2 tbsp extra virgin olive oil
1 tbsp apple cider vinegar
½ tsp Himalayan salt

To make the dressing, squash the raspberries with a fork. Stir in the remaining ingredients or combine in a mini travel blender.

Cut the thick core off the cabbage. Slice or grate the leaves into ultra-thin strips. Put the cabbage strips in a bowl, pour over the dressing and massage it into the leaves. At this point you can transfer the mixture to glass jars and store it in the refrigerator for up to 7 days.

To serve, arrange the spinach and sprouts on 4 plates to make a bed for the strips of cabbage, then pile the cabbage on top.

Cucumber & Sea

— SERVES 2

This ultra-healthy recipe is one I make often for lunch, dinner, parties or picnics. It can be used as a filling for a wrap or a sandwich and is lovely over a Sunburger (see p.78) or with Pesto (see p.106). Yep, it goes with anything and everything, because it's that delicious.

25g (1oz) wakame seaweed
1 large seedless cucumber, thinly sliced
  with a mandoline or potato peeler
70g (2½oz) pumpkin seeds, soaked for
  4–6 hours
fresh herbs (such as dill and parsley)
  and sliced spring onion, to taste

For the dressing:
4 tbsp extra virgin olive oil
2 tbsp toasted sesame oil
2 tbsp balsamic vinegar
2.5cm (1in) root ginger, grated
1 tbsp apple cider vinegar
1 tbsp white miso paste
1 tbsp raw honey
juice of 1 lime
Himalayan salt, to taste

Process the dressing ingredients in a mini travel blender and set aside. Immerse the seaweed in a bowl of boiling water and set it aside for 5–10 minutes to soften. Then drain, rinse under cold water and pat dry. Remove any tough ribs and thinly slice. Arrange the cucumber strips on a serving plate, twisting them attractively. Sprinkle with wakame, seeds, herbs and onion, then drizzle with the dressing.

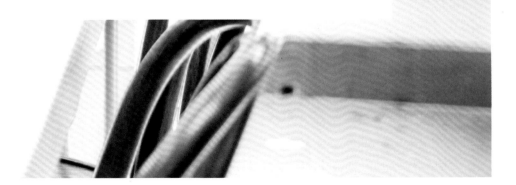

CHAPTER 4

Main Meals

When it comes to raw food, it is the issue of main meals that stops many from sticking to the path. I'm here to show you that you don't need a dehydrator for every meal, or a lot of hours of preparation to have a winning dish, and that you don't need to worry about whether your spouse or your children are going to like the results. These meals are easy to prepare and have been tried, tested and approved by the wonderful visitors – of all ages – to Tanya's Café.

Sunburgers

— SERVES 5-7

On the last day of my first Ecuadorian retreat, I threw a bunch of remaining ingredients into a food processor and the result was these delicious burgers. I even surprised myself with how many I ate – usually, when developing recipes, I taste test as I go along and, by the time the meal is ready, I'm too full to eat it. So these burgers come with a warning – they are very moreish!

For the patty:

240g (8½oz) sunflower seeds, soaked for 4-6 hours

130g (4½oz) cashew nuts, soaked for 4-6 hours

100g (3oz) sundried tomatoes, soaked for 4-6 hours

80ml (3fl oz) sundried tomato soaking water

1 large white onion, quartered or roughly chopped

10g (¼oz) dill fronds and finer stalks, plus extra to garnish

½ tsp ground black pepper

Serve with:

Onion Bread (see p.110) (optional)

lettuce leaves

slices of onion, tomato and avocado

Ketchup (see p.107) or Ranch Dressing (see p.107)

Combine all the patty ingredients in a food processor with an S-blade – you are looking for a thick, grainy paste, so keep pulsing and scraping down the processor bowl with a spatula as you go until you achieve the right texture.

Using a burger press, a Metric Wonder Cup or simply your hands, form 14–15 patties with the paste, each about 3cm (1¼in) thick. Arrange them, spaced out, over mesh trays and dehydrate for 10 hours at 48°C. Wiggle the patties to unstick them from the tray, turn them over and dehydrate for another 6–12 hours, depending on how dense and dry you like your burgers to be.

Serve on onion bread, if using, with lettuce, some onion and tomato sliced into rings and slices of avocado, with your favourite sauce scooped over the top and a few dill fronds to garnish. If you're not eating the burgers straight away, store them in the refrigerator at all times.

TANYA'S
TOP TIP

If the mixture is too runny when you're moulding the patties, you might like to dehydrate it in blobs for 4 hours, then re-form the patties.

Stuffed Peppers

Stuffed Peppers

— SERVES 3

Stuffed peppers are so easy and quick to make, they look amazing as a starter, main meal, snack or canapé and will never go out of style. They can be stuffed with virtually anything, from leftover sauces and fillings to salads, but the combination of pine nuts and sundried tomatoes does it for me.

3 Romano or 9 pimiento peppers

For the stuffing:
150g (5½oz) sundried tomatoes
150g (5½oz) pine nuts
135g (4¾oz) pumpkin seeds, soaked for
 4–6 hours
120g (4¼oz) sunflower seeds, soaked for
 4–6 hours
150g (5½oz) cherry tomatoes, chopped
2 tbsp extra virgin olive oil
2 tbsp balsamic vinegar
1 tsp finely chopped rosemary

To prepare the stuffing, pulverise the sundried tomatoes in a food processor. Add the remaining ingredients and pulse until well combined. Scrape any mixture that is stuck on the side of the bowl down onto the blade, then process again. Go steady on the pulse button as the stuffing is a whole lot more exciting with a bit of texture, and once it's a paste, there is no going back.

Halve the peppers lengthwise to resemble boats, leaving the stalks intact. Discard the seeds.

Spoon the filling into the peppers, distribute them over mesh trays and dehydrate at 48°C for 5 hours. Serve warm, straight from the dehydrator, or at room temperature.

Alkalising Pesto Pasta

— SERVES 4

Substitute courgettes for traditional pasta for a gluten-free, low-calorie, water-rich meal. Add garlic, lemon, basil and nuts in the mix and you have an immune-boosting, alkalising, protein-packed combo, with a drizzle of olive oil to protect your heart. Serve with any salady bits you like.

For the noodles:
4 medium courgettes, spiralised

For the pesto sauce:
70g (2½oz) basil, packed tightly
110g (4oz) spinach
75g (2¾oz) pine nuts
75g (2¾oz) Brazil nuts
3 garlic cloves, minced

⅓ tsp Himalayan salt
240ml (8¼fl oz) extra virgin olive oil (or
 flaxseed oil)
juice of 3 limes

Serve with:
cherry tomatoes, marinated mushrooms,
 sauerkraut, salad greens – anything
 goes!

Blend all the pesto ingredients except the oil and lime juice in a food processor until finely ground. Add the oil and lime juice and pulse into a sauce. Pour the pesto over the spiralised courgettes and stir it through. Serve immediately, or leave the noodles to marinate in the juices.

Ravioli

— SERVES 4

This ravioli is so flavoursome, light and fancy, it'll win over all your dinner party guests. But why wait for guests when you can celebrate being alive right now? Preparing a good meal for yourself is one way to practise some self-love – and a highly effective way, at that. For instance, for this particular dish, you will activate nuts to give them (and your cells) life, then, as with other dishes, you will shop for your groceries, giving them (and your health) attention, you will touch living food with your bare hands, exchanging energy with it. And after all of your efforts, you will devote time to enjoying the meal, chewing it thoroughly and tasting it fully, which will do wonders for your digestion.

2 round courgettes or pears
1 quantity Soured Cream (see p.106)

For the filling:
150g (5½oz) portobello mushrooms, peeled
150g (5½oz) oyster mushrooms
2 tbsp liquid aminos
2 tbsp balsamic vinegar
2 tbsp apple cider vinegar
1 garlic clove, minced
180g (6¼oz) sunflower seeds, soaked for 4–6 hours
1 tbsp white miso paste

For the pistachio pesto:
70g (2½oz) basil leaves
100g (3oz) unsalted hulled pistachio nuts
2 garlic cloves, minced
2 tbsp nutritional yeast
⅓ tsp Himalayan salt
180ml (6fl oz) extra virgin olive oil
juice of 1 lemon

First of all, prepare the mushrooms so they can be left to marinate. Once you've peeled off the skins of the portobello mushrooms, slice them and the oyster mushrooms very thinly. Transfer to a large bowl and add the remaining filling ingredients except for the sunflower seeds and miso paste. Stir to mix the juices into the mushrooms, then set aside at room temperature to marinate. After the mushrooms have marinated for 30–60 minutes, transfer the contents of the bowl to the food processor, add the seeds and the miso and process to a chunky paste.

To prepare the pesto, combine all the ingredients in a high-speed blender until broken down but not smooth.

Using the finest possible setting on a mandoline, slice the courgettes or pears, from the bases upwards, into fine round slices – they should be thin enough to bend freely and be folded in half. If the courgette is too wide for the mandoline, slice an edge off to fit. Lay the round slices onto a nonstick pan, scoop a spoonful of mushroom filling on 1 side of each slice, then fold the slices in half over the filling.

Assemble the prepared ravioli onto plates, drizzle with the pistachio pesto and serve.

Four-layer Lasagne

— SERVES 6–9

If you have a blender or food processor, you can most definitely rock out a raw-food lasagne. Once prepared with the soaked ingredients, you could assemble the dish and be eating it within just 30 minutes! Oh, and did I mention how sweet, tangy, creamy, refreshing and delicious this meal is?

3 medium courgettes
2 medium tomatoes, thinly sliced
1 quantity Pesto (see p.106)
basil leaves or edible flowers

For the mushroom layer:
250g (9oz) portobello mushrooms, peeled
3 tbsp tamari
2 tbsp extra virgin olive oil
2 tbsp apple cider vinegar
50g (1¾oz) walnuts, soaked for 4–6 hours
50g (1¾oz) sundried tomatoes, soaked for 4–6 hours
2 tbsp white miso paste
2 tsp mixed Italian herbs
1 tsp paprika

For the 'cheese' layer:
280g (10oz) macadamia nuts
25g (1oz) nutritional yeast
juice of 2 lemons
4 garlic cloves
½ tsp Himalayan salt
240ml (8¼fl oz) water, plus more as needed

For the tomato paste layer:
150g (5½oz) sundried tomatoes, soaked in warm water for 4–6 hours
3 medium tomatoes, roughly chopped
5 pitted dates, soaked for 4–6 hours
2 tbsp mixed Italian herbs

Unless you have plenty of time for preparation, follow this method in the order given to make the lasagne within 30 minutes. First, make a start on the mushroom layer. Thinly slice the mushrooms, place them in a bowl and stir in the tamari, oil and vinegar. Set aside to marinate, stirring every 10 minutes to ensure the liquids penetrate the mushrooms evenly.

Using a mandoline on the finest setting, a knife or a potato peeler, thinly slice the courgettes along their lengths into long, flat sheets.

Blend the 'cheese' layer ingredients in a blender until smooth. If you don't have a high-powered blender, you may need more water, but add it in small amounts and stop once the mixture is smooth. Or use a food processor instead – your mixture will have more texture and bite. Scoop the mixture into a bowl. Good news – there's no need to wash the blender between preparing the different sauces – it's all going into the same meal anyway.

Put all the tomato paste layer ingredients into the blender and blend, using the tamper, until they are well combined. Scoop out the mixture into a bowl.

Strain the marinated mushrooms and transfer to the blender, add the remaining mushroom-layer ingredients and blend to a chunky paste.

You'll need a 40 x 27cm (16 x 10¾n) rectangular ovenproof roasting dish in which to prepare the lasagne. To layer the lasagne, first cover the base of the dish with courgette sheets, overlapping them slightly so there are no gaps. Spread over this a layer of tomato paste, then add another layer of courgette sheets. Spread with a layer of cheese, then more courgettes. Follow with a layer of mushroom, the tomato slices, then more courgettes and, finally, a pesto layer. If you have courgette sheets remaining, cover the top with those. Thin layers of sauce are best, both for the enjoyment of this dish and for it to hold together well, so if you find you have plenty of sauce to work with, make it an 8-layer lasagne instead of a 4-layer one.

Slice the lasagne with a sharp knife and scoop out each piece with a fish slice. Sprinkle with basil leaves or edible flowers to serve.

Nut-free Pizza with 'Roasted' Veg

— *SERVES 4–8*

Who doesn't love pizza? It was the first thing I made in a dehydrator (I know I'm not the only one), as I was eager to make a raw pizza my husband, Elliot, would approve of. After years of experimenting to create the perfect base, it's this very dish that gets him booking lunch meetings at Tanya's Café.

1 large carrot, sliced

1 yellow pepper, deseeded and sliced

1 red onion, sliced

300g (10½oz) cherry tomatoes, quartered

200g (7oz) button mushrooms, quartered

your favourite seasonal vegetables, sliced/chopped (optional)

½ quantity Ketchup (see p.107)

½ quantity Creamy Cultured Cheese (see p.163)

olives and basil leaves, to serve

For the rub:

160ml (5½fl oz) extra virgin olive oil

1 tbsp dried mixed Italian herbs

2 tsp garlic powder

2 tsp ground cumin

1 tsp paprika

1 tsp chilli powder or ½ tsp cayenne pepper

½ tsp Himalayan salt

For the pizza bases (makes 2):

300g (10½oz) courgettes, peeled and chopped

1 white onion, chopped

4 tbsp extra virgin olive oil

4 tbsp lemon juice

2 tbsp nutritional yeast

1 tsp Himalayan salt

240ml (8¼fl oz) gluten-free porridge oat flakes

130g (4½oz) coconut flour

100g (3oz) ground flaxseeds

To make the pizza bases, combine all the ingredients, except the porridge oats, coconut flour and flax, in a food processor until smooth. Add these remaining ingredients and process again to combine. Divide the mixture in half, place each portion on a Teflex sheet and use a soft spatula to manipulate each mound into a classic round pizza-base shape. I aim for a thickness of approximately 1cm (½in), but you can make your pizza bases even thinner to speed up the dehydration process. Tidy up the edges, making them as smooth or as rugged as your heart desires.

Dehydrate at 48°C for 8 hours. Flip over the bases onto mesh trays, peel off the Teflex sheets and return to the dehydrator for another 12 hours.

Combine the rub ingredients in a bowl, add the prepared vegetables and stir well with a wooden spoon until the veggies are evenly coated. Distribute the coated vegetables across Teflex sheets and dehydrate at 48°C for 2–4 hours. Set the timer, and check the veggies from time to time – you don't want to be chewing on dried-up snacks. Instead, you want veggies with body and bite.

Assemble the pizza just before serving, so the ketchup doesn't moisten the bases too much and make them soggy. Smear ketchup over the bases. Slice each base into 4, 6 or 8 pieces. Load the slices with the veggies, scoop on blobs of the creamy cheese, top with olives and sprinkle with basil leaves.

TANYA'S TOP TIP

If you would like a crispier crust, make it thinner rather than dehydrating it for a longer period of time. I would avoid dehydrating a 1cm (½in) crust for any more than 24 hours, as it will start to become quite solid and tough to chew.

From left: Spaghetti Nut Balls, Cannelloni (see p.90)

Spaghetti Nut Balls

— SERVES 6-9

Let's indulge in a bit of trivia – did the Chinese first invent noodles, or was it the Italians with spaghetti? There's so much debate around this one. According to Greek mythology, it was the Greek God Vulcan who invented a device that produced strings of dough! Whatever the answer, I reckon that if something as well-loved as the cooked noodle can remain popular worldwide for so long, then enthusiasm for its mega-healthy look- and taste-alike version is surely here to stay.

250g (9oz) portobello mushrooms, peeled and thinly sliced
100g (3oz) walnuts, soaked for 4–6 hours
135g (4¾oz) pumpkin seeds, soaked for 4–6 hours
2 carrots (about 170g/6oz), grated
½ white onion, chopped
1 tbsp dried mixed Italian herbs
35–50g (1¼–1¾oz) ground flaxseeds
2 courgettes, spiralised
basil, to garnish

For the mushroom marinade:
3 tbsp liquid aminos
2 tbsp apple cider vinegar
2 tbsp lemon juice
2 garlic cloves, minced

For the Bolognese sauce:
3 tomatoes, chopped
20 dry sundried tomato halves, soaked for 4–6 hours, or 250g (9oz) jar oil-soaked sundried tomatoes, drained
1 red pepper, deseeded and chopped
juice of 1 lemon
20g (¾oz) fresh basil
3 tbsp Date Paste (see p.108) or 3 Medjool dates, pitted
3 tbsp extra virgin olive oil
1 tbsp dried mixed Italian herbs
½ tbsp garlic powder

Put the sliced mushrooms in a bowl, add the marinade ingredients and stir well. Set aside for a minimum of 1 hour and, ideally, for 6 hours.

Rinse the soaked walnuts and put them, along with the pumpkin seeds, carrot, onion and Italian herbs, into a food processor with an S-blade. You will also add ground flaxseed, but the amount you need depends on how much of the mushroom marinade is left. The quantity of marinade that remains will depend on the length of time for which you marinated the mushrooms. If there is only a small amount, add only 35g (1¼oz) ground flaxseed, but if your mushrooms are drowning in liquid, add the remaining amount. Finally, add the mushrooms and their marinade. Pulse until the mixture is well combined, then scrape down the side of the processor bowl and process the mixture to a paste.

Using your hands, roll the mixture into balls of any size you like, but note that the larger they are, the longer it will take to dehydrate them. Distribute the balls across dehydrator mesh trays and dehydrate at 48°C for 8 hours.

Pop all the Bolognese sauce ingredients into a food processor and blend into a sauce.

Create a bed of courgette noodles on each plate. Add a generous helping of the sauce over the noodles, then assemble a few nut balls on top and garnish with basil leaves to serve. Alternatively, mix the noodles with the sauce and set aside to soak up the flavours for 1 hour before serving with the nut balls. This version is less photogenic, but the noodles do taste even better!

TANYA'S TOP TIP

If you don't have a spiraliser, you can slice the courgettes lengthwise, as thinly as possible, then cut these slices into narrow strips to resemble noodles. Or try using a grater or a potato peeler to achieve noodle shapes.

Cannelloni

— SERVES 4

This dish is beautiful, in terms of how it looks, how it tastes and how it makes you feel, with the added bonus of being a quickie to make. Cannelloni is always popular at Tanya's Café. Perhaps the element of surprise – not knowing what's inside the tubes – gives the dish an irresistible fun factor. The filling recipe given here is delicious, but try out either the mushroom mixture from Four-layer Lasagne (see p.85) or the one from Spaghetti Nut Balls (see p.89).

2 courgettes
extra virgin olive oil
Himalayan salt

For the filling:
75g (2¾oz) almonds, soaked for
  6–8 hours
55g (2oz) pecan nuts, soaked for
  4–6 hours
60g (2oz) sunflower seeds, soaked for
  4–6 hours
70g (2½oz) pumpkin seeds, soaked
  for 4–6 hours
2 tbsp tamari
1 tbsp Date Paste (see p.108) or 1 Medjool
  date, pitted
1 tbsp dried mixed Italian herbs
1 tsp nutmeg
½ tsp ground cinnamon

For the sauce:
1 quantity Bolognese sauce (see p.89)

Use the finest setting on a mandoline to slice the courgettes lengthwise. The resulting slices should be thin and pliable. Arrange ¼ of these slices on a chopping board, side by side but with the edges overlapping slightly, to create 1 large sheet that is roughly the size of an A4 sheet of paper.

Put all the filling ingredients in a food processor and use the pulse setting to break up the nuts and seeds until they are completely broken down and the mixture becomes a paste.

Spoon ¼ of the filling across 1 of the longer edges of the courgette sheet. Now roll the sheet over the filling to enclose it, then continue rolling until you reach the end of the courgette sheet. Slice the large roll into 3 smaller rolls. Brush a little oil on top of the cannelloni, sprinkle with salt and set aside this single serving.

Repeat the layering and rolling process described above to create 3 further servings of cannelloni.

Scoop a large helping of Bolognese onto 4 plates, arrange 3 cannelloni tubes on top of each portion of sauce and serve immediately.

TANYA'S
TOP TIP

If you don't have a mandoline, use a potato peeler to create the thin courgette slices required for this dish. Depending on the width of your peeler, the slices may be narrow, but this won't matter when you put them together into sheets.

Mushroom Strogonov

— SERVES 3

If you are craving meat, most likely it is the texture of it that you desire, and it's possible that you're deficient in iron. The body is skilled at giving us clues about what it needs through cravings, but nature is excellent at offering plant-based options to keep us strong and healthy. Mushrooms can hit the spot in the meaty texture department, and they also provide iron and defence against bacterial invasion, and are one of the few foods that allow us to increase our vitamin D levels through diet.

500g (1lb 2oz) large portobello
 mushrooms, peeled
130g (4½oz) cashew nuts, soaked for
 4-6 hours
2 tbsp white miso paste

For the marinade:
80ml (3fl oz) warm water
5 tbsp tamari
3 tbsp apple cider vinegar
2 garlic cloves, minced
1½ tbsp thyme leaves
1½ tsp paprika

Serve with:
1 quantity Creamy Cauliflower Mash
 (see p.102)
micro greens

Slice the mushrooms to your preferred thickness. If you have less time to prepare the dish, make the slices small, as smaller slices will absorb the marinade quickly.

Place the mushroom slices in a bowl, add the marinade ingredients and stir well. Leave to marinate at room temperature for a minimum of 1 hour, stirring occasionally.

Pour the marinade into a blender, add the cashews and miso and blend until creamy. Transfer to a bowl, add the marinated mushrooms and stir the mixture well.

Serve the mushroom mixture on a bed of cauliflower mash, sprinkled with micro greens.

TANYA'S
TOP TIP

Mushrooms absorb whatever is in the environment they grow in, whether it is good or bad. It's therefore very important that you eat only organically grown mushrooms to avoid any air and water pollutants, not to mention heavy metals.

Clockwise from top left: Everyday Green juice (see p.24), Minty Tzatziki Dip (see p.138), The Healer juice (see p.25), Peanut Butter Cups (see p.151), strawberries dipped in chocolate, Falafel, Tabouli, Smoked Pepper Hummus (see p.105)

Falafel Feast

— SERVES 6-8

This delicious meal has 'family' written all over it. It's designed for sharing, passing, spilling, smudging, crumbing, laughing and creating memories. Furthermore, it's full of nutrients. Many people seem to find raw chickpeas difficult to digest, so I use sunflower seeds instead.

For the falafels:
240g (8½oz) sunflower seeds, soaked for
  4-6 hours
200g (7oz) carrots, grated
4 celery sticks, chopped
50g (1¾oz) ground flaxseeds
juice of 1½ lemons
15g (½oz) parsley leaves
10g (¼oz) dill fronds
3 tbsp liquid aminos
3 tbsp Date Paste (see p.108) or
  75g (2¾oz) pitted dates, soaked
  for 4-6 hours
2 tbsp raw tahini
2 tbsp ground cumin
1 tbsp garlic powder

For the tabouli:
250g (9oz) cauliflower florets
¼ tsp Himalayan salt
¼ tsp ground black pepper
2 spring onions, thinly sliced
2 large tomatoes, finely chopped
4 tbsp lemon juice
60g (2oz) parsley, finely chopped
10g (¼oz) mint leaves, finely chopped
4 tbsp extra virgin olive oil
1 tsp mixed spice
90g (3oz) pitted olives, chopped

Serve with:
1 quantity Hummus (see p.105)
1 quantity Minty Tzatziki (see p.138)
lettuce leaves and lime wedges

To make the falafels, put the sunflower seeds, carrot and celery in a food processor and blend to a runny paste. Add the remaining falafel ingredients and pulse until everything is broken down and the mixture is well combined. You may need to scrape down the side of the bowl with a spatula a few times.

Using your hands, roll the mixture into 3cm (1¼in) balls. Arrange these over 2 dehydrator mesh trays, leaving space between each ball so that they dry evenly. Dehydrate at 48°C for 10 hours. If you want the falafels to be extra dry (to eat on the road or to keep them for longer), dehydrate the balls for 30 hours.

To make the tabouli, pulse the cauliflower in a food processor until it resembles rice or couscous. Transfer to a large bowl, sprinkle evenly with the remaining tabouli ingredients and stir. Serve it immediately, because tabouli is best when it's fresh.

Serve the falafels as a feast, with dishes of tabouli, hummus and tzatziki alongside, with lettuce and lime wedges for squeezing.

TANYA'S TOP TIP

When making tabouli, mix the salt and pepper with the spring onions before adding to the mixture, to bring out the sweet juices of the onion.

Nori Wraps with Pickled Ginger

— SERVES 2-4

This wrap has been one of my go-to lunches for as long as I've been working with raw food. The filling is made with sunflower seeds, which I have always loved. In Russia, sweet old grannies (including my own) would sell newspaper cones filled with seeds harvested from flowers they grew themselves. I recall picking one up on my way back from school, leaving a trail of black shells all the way home. Now I know how much vitamin E, selenium, manganese, phosphorus, magnesium and copper are in each seed, I'm happy that this wonder snack was always readily available in my family.

4 nori sheets

For the pickled ginger:
100g (3oz) root ginger
2 tbsp apple cider vinegar
1 tbsp raw honey or 2 tbsp agave nectar
juice of 1 lemon
pinch of Himalayan salt

For the 'rice':
180g (6¼oz) sunflower seeds, soaked for
  4-6 hours
2 tbsp white miso paste

For the filling:
1 carrot, cut into thin strips
1 avocado, sliced
1 apple, cored and cut into thin strips
½ red pepper, deseeded and cut into thin
  strips
your choice of seasonal vegetables,
  cut into thin strips
15g (½oz) parsley leaves or sprouts, or
  to taste

Start by preparing the pickled ginger. Peel the ginger and slice it very thinly using a mandoline. Place it in a bowl, add the remaining pickle ingredients and leave to infuse at room temperature for a minimum of 8 hours and, ideally, for 48 hours. (The pickled ginger can be stored, refrigerated, in an airtight container for up to 6 weeks.)

Process the 'rice' ingredients in a food processor to a chunky paste, scraping down the side of the jug for even blending. Transfer to a bowl and divide the paste into 4 portions.

To make the rolls, position 1 nori sheet, with the shiny side facing down, on a chopping board. Spoon 1 portion of the 'rice' paste in a long band along one end of the sheet, slightly in from the edge. Remember that this band will provide a bed for the vegetable strips, so ensure it is a good deal wider than the bundle of veggie strips you're planning to put on top.

Divide the prepared filling veggies into 4 portions and load 1 portion onto the band of 'rice'. If the veggies are cut in consistent widths, and you lay them evenly across the band, there won't be any bulges in the wrap once it is rolled.

Carefully roll the end of the nori sheet over the filling to roll up the sushi wrap – it works best if you push the roll away from you. Just before you complete the roll, run your dampened fingers or a slice of tomato along the free end of the nori sheet, then push the roll over the dampened edge to seal it. Repeat with the remaining nori sheets, 'rice' paste and filling.

It's not necessary to cut the rolls but, if you prefer to, use a super-sharp knife to slice the wraps into sushi rolls. Serve with the pickled ginger. Remember to cleanse your palate with a little pickled ginger between each roll – this is how it is eaten traditionally.

Thai Curry Kelp Noodles

— SERVES 4

When my eBook *Nourished – Comforting Raw Foods for Winter* came out, it was this dish that inspired bloggers to claim that this recipe alone was worth the price of the entire book! Not only is the curry delicious, it is bursting with nutrients. Dry coconut comes with fibre, iron, protein and zinc – the ideal combo for healthy tissues, blood and bones and for gorgeous skin. Kelp noodles are well known for their high iodine content, which plays a key role in metabolism and thyroid function.

For the curry sauce:
1 litre (1¾ pints) coconut milk (see tip, below)
200g (7oz) cashew nuts, soaked for 4–6 hours
zest and juice of 2 limes
4 tbsp tamari
4 tbsp Date Paste (see p.108) or 75g (2¾oz) pitted dates, soaked for 4–6 hours
2 garlic cloves
1½ green chillies
2.5cm (1in) root ginger
1 tbsp ground cumin
2 tsp ground coriander

For the noodles:
340g (11¾oz) pack of kelp noodles
2 courgettes, spiralised

Optional extras:
½ quantity 'Roasted' Veg (see p.86) or Hearty Kale Salad (see p.63)
sugar snap peas, thinly sliced
baby corn, thinly sliced
parsley leaves
dried chilli flakes

Put the coconut milk into a blender, add the remaining curry sauce ingredients and blend on a high setting. Keep the motor running for 2–3 minutes if you would like to serve the sauce warm.

Put the noodles and spiralised courgettes in a bowl. Add the curry sauce and stir it through. Leave the kelp and courgette noodles to sit in the sauce for at least 10 minutes to give them time to soften.

Serve the curry in bowls with either 'roasted' veggies or on a bed of kale salad. Sprinkle each serving with optional veggies for an authentically Thai dish, and with the parsley leaves and chilli flakes for added colour and flavour.

TANYA'S TOP TIP

You can prepare coconut milk by following the method for making nut or seed milk (see p.33), substituting coconut flesh or desiccated coconut for the nuts or seeds. For this recipe, I blend either the flesh from 1 brown coconut or 135g (4¾oz) desiccated coconut with 1 litre (1¾ pints) water in a blender, then strain.

Taco Feast

— SERVES 6

For the raw food enthusiast, lettuce or cabbage leaves make the ideal receptacles for guacamole, salsa and soured cream, but if you want to show off your wizard dehydration skills, have a go at making these tasty raw taco shells to give your guests a glorious Mexican feast.

For the taco shells (makes 10–12):
280g (10oz) corn kernels, defrosted
120g (4¼oz) sunflower seeds, soaked
  for 4–6 hours
1 medium tomato, roughly chopped
1 yellow pepper, deseeded and chopped
juice of 1 lemon
50g (1¾oz) ground flaxseeds
55g (2oz) white sesame seeds
90g (3oz) chia seeds
1 tbsp ground cumin
1 tbsp ground coriander
1 tbsp garlic powder
water, as needed

For the filling:
2 tbsp liquid aminos
1 tbsp apple cider vinegar
1 tbsp lemon juice
150g (5½oz) oyster mushrooms, sliced
180g (6¼oz) sunflower seeds, soaked for
  4–6 hours
100g (3oz) sundried tomatoes, soaked
  for 4–6 hours, plus 3 tbsp of the
  soaking water
3 tbsp Date Paste (see p.108) or
  3 Medjool dates, pitted
2 tbsp extra virgin olive oil
1 tbsp dark miso paste
2 tsp ground cumin
2 tsp ground coriander
2 tsp garlic powder
1 tsp chilli powder

Serve with:
Guacamole (see p.105)
Pineapple Salsa (see p.64)
Soured Cream (see p.106)

To make the taco shells, put all the ingredients into a food processor and blend until well combined, adding just enough water to produce a soft paste. (If you have a powerful food processor, you may not need to add any water at all.)

Divide the mixture into 10–12 equal portions and dollop these across 2–3 Teflex sheets. Spread out each portion into a thin round. Dehydrate at 48°C for 10 hours. Peel the leathers off the sheets and transfer onto mesh trays.

Fold up the sides of each leather to resemble a taco shell. They are likely to be too flimsy to hold their shapes during further dehydration, so scrunch up kitchen foil into tubes and place 1 tube inside each shell to help it hold its shape. Alternatively,

you can drape the shapes over the sides of plastic food containers and place the containers straight into the dehydrator. Dehydrate on mesh trays (or on the plastic containers) for at least a further 14 hours. You can store the finished taco shells in an airtight container for up to 4 weeks.

To make the filling, mix the liquid aminos, vinegar and lemon juice in a bowl, add the sliced mushrooms and stir well. Leave to marinate for a minimum of 1 hour and, ideally, for 3 hours.

Put the mushrooms along with their marinade into a food processor with the remaining filling ingredients. Blend thoroughly to a thick paste. You may need to scrape down the side of the food processor with a spatula a few times during the process.

Serve the taco shells in a large bowl, with the dips and taco filling in separate bowls with spoons, so that everyone can help themselves.

CHAPTER 5

Sauces & Sides

If you really think about what finishes a burger or makes a sandwich great, it's usually all down to the condiments. Having a few good recipes for sauces up your sleeve allows you to transform all your meals or snacks into the most insane delicacies. A good rule of thumb to follow is to apply the FASS rule to every sauce you create – include a little Fat (oil), Acid (a tangy acid, such as lemon, not pH acid), Sweet (even peppers can be sweet) and Salt.

Creamy Cauliflower Mash

—SERVES 3

Although I won't start telling you that raw cauliflower mash tastes just like cooked mashed potatoes, I can assure you that this is one surprisingly delightful dish. And, of course, it contains no starch to weigh you down but, instead, is full of plenty of cleansing, immune-boosting, heart-strengthening, anti-inflammatory goodness, which this cruciferous vegetable is so well known for.

130g (4½oz) cashew nuts, soaked for 4–6 hours
180ml (6fl oz) warm water
1 small cauliflower, chopped
4 tbsp extra virgin olive oil
4 tbsp nutritional yeast

3 tbsp manuka honey
2 tbsp lemon juice
2 garlic cloves, minced
1 tsp paprika
Himalayan salt and ground black pepper, to taste

First, blend the cashews and water to make a cream. Add the remaining ingredients to the blender and blend until smooth, using the tamper or the pulse button. Check the seasoning and adjust if necessary.

Warming Avocado Fries

— SERVES 2

These comforting 'breaded' avocado strips are called fries, but really there is no comparison to cooked fries, except that they are meant to be served as a side dish. However, avocado fries taste so out-of-this-world, they can easily become the main attraction. I find that, no matter what you serve them with, they are often eaten up well before anything else is even touched.

1 large ripe avocado (or 2 small)

For the coating:
50g (1¾oz) ground flaxseeds
1 tbsp nutritional yeast
2 tsp garlic powder
1 tsp Himalayan salt
1 tsp dried oregano
½ tsp cayenne pepper

Cut the avocado in half lengthwise and remove the stone. While the flesh is still in the skin, use a tip of a knife to slice it into long strips that resemble fries in shape. Use a spoon to scoop out the strips.

Mix the coating ingredients in a bowl, then roll the avocado strips in the flax breading to coat them. Transfer to a plate or bowl to serve.

TANYA'S TOP TIP

To serve these fries warm, put them on a baking tray on baking paper. Preheat the oven to 100°C, then switch it off and pop in the fries until warm. This allows the avocado oils to soak into the breading, which is delicious. And, wahoo – you can still use that oven!

Clockwise from top left: Soured Cream (see p.106), Caramelised Onions (see p.110), Guacamole (see p.105), Creamy Cauliflower Mash, Warming Avocado Fries, Ketchup (see p.107)

Smoked Pepper Hummus

Smoked Pepper Hummus

– SERVES 4

When you cook chickpeas (or anything), the contained carbohydrates turn to sugar, so the cooked result will always be sweeter than the raw version – unless you load your raw dishes with sugar, which isn't really that desirable. I haven't tasted a raw chickpea hummus that blew me away, but ditch the chickpeas in favour of courgettes and it's suddenly a different story.

1 large courgette, chopped
60g (2oz) sunflower seeds, soaked for 4–6 hours
50g (1¾oz) sundried tomatoes, soaked for 2–4 hours
90g (3oz) raw tahini
2 tbsp extra virgin olive oil

3 tbsp lemon juice
3 tbsp water
1 tbsp sweet smoked paprika
1 heaped tsp ground cumin
½ tsp Himalayan salt (use only if your sundried tomatoes are not preserved in salt)

Put all the ingredients in a high-powered blender and blend to a rich, thick consistency.

Transfer the mixture to an airtight container and refrigerate immediately. Store, refrigerated, for up to 5 days.

Guacamole

– SERVES 3

It's hard now to imagine that I lived without avocados for the first 11 years of my life. We'd never heard of them in Vladivostok and my parents didn't even taste them until they were the age I am now. It's not as if avocados aren't easy enough to eat all on their own, but you can also mash them up into this simple yet perfect guacamole.

2 ripe avocados
juice of 1 lime
1 tsp ground cumin
1 tsp garlic powder
½ tsp Himalayan salt
pinch of cayenne pepper
1 plum tomato, finely chopped
½ white onion, finely chopped
15g (½ oz) fresh coriander, chopped

Scoop out the avocado flesh into a bowl. Squeeze over the lime juice and sprinkle over the dry powders. Use a fork to squash and mix the ingredients until there are no obvious chunks. Stir in the remaining ingredients and you're done! Serve immediately. You can keep the dip, refrigerated, for up to 2 days, but it browns with each hour so won't look as great as when fresh.

TANYA'S TOP TIP

To ripen avocados at home within 3 days, seal them in a brown paper bag with bananas, tomatoes or apples, or place the unripe avocados in a fruit bowl surrounded with these fruits. They emit ethylene gas, which speeds up ripening.

Pesto

— MAKES ENOUGH TO FILL A 500ML (18FL OZ) JAR

Pesto seems to be much loved no matter where in the world I travel, but perhaps that's because I chase the sun and pesto is the epitome of summer. Did you know that you can freeze pesto when basil is readily available and at its best? You can store it for up to two whopping years in your freezer.

100g (3oz) fresh basil
140g (5oz) macadamia nuts
150g (5½oz) pine nuts
80ml (3fl oz) extra virgin olive oil
juice of 2 lemons
3 garlic cloves, minced
1 tsp Himalayan salt

Discard the thickest basil stalks, then put the basil in a food processor with an S-blade. Add the macadamia nuts and pulse until they are slightly broken down. Add the pine nuts and pulse until they appear chopped.

Scrape down the side of the processor bowl, add the remaining ingredients and pulse again until the pesto has your desired texture. Transfer to an airtight container and refrigerate for up to 3 months.

Soured Cream

— MAKES ENOUGH TO FILL A 300ML (½PINT) JAR

I make this soured cream on a weekly basis to see me through my healthy week. But sometimes, I choose to make up a big batch just once every two or even three weeks – it just tastes better and better with time. It will keep in the refrigerator for three weeks, is useful in so many recipes and, once you've soaked the nuts, takes barely any time to make, so it's worth making it in bulk to keep.

140g (5oz) macadamia nuts, cashew nuts
  or a mix of both, soaked for 4–8 hours
120ml (4fl oz) water
juice of 2 limes
2 garlic cloves
⅓ tsp Himalayan salt
pinch of ground black pepper

Put all the ingredients in a blender and blend on a high speed setting until creamy. Transfer the mixture to an airtight container and refrigerate until ready to use.

Ketchup

– MAKES ENOUGH TO FILL A 1 LITRE (1¾ PINTS) JAR

If your family loves a good ketchup, this one is the tastiest healthy alternative there is! Fill the empty bottle of the family's favoured brand with this one and don't tell them – they might never notice.

150g (5½oz) sundried tomatoes, soaked for 4-6 hours, plus 120ml (4fl oz) tomato soaking water

150g (5½oz) pitted dates, soaked for 4-6 hours, plus 120ml (4fl oz) date soaking water

300g (10½oz) ripe tomatoes, chopped

4 tbsp apple cider vinegar
4 tbsp balsamic vinegar
10g (¼oz) nutritional yeast
2 tbsp liquid aminos
2 garlic cloves
½ tsp paprika
Himalayan salt and black pepper, to taste

Put all the ingredients in a blender and blend with a tamper until you have a thick, smooth paste. You may need to pulse a few times and stop to check and adjust the seasoning. Transfer to an airtight container and refrigerate for up to 4 weeks.

Ranch Dressing

– MAKES ENOUGH TO FILL A 500ML (18FL OZ) JAR

I took on my American friends' challenge to make a raw ranch dressing and, in turn, fulfilled my own quest to consume more onions. Now this could possibly be my favourite dip of all time.

130g (4½oz) cashew nuts, soaked for 4-6 hours
120ml (4fl oz) lemon juice
80ml (3fl oz) liquid aminos
4 tbsp apple cider vinegar
4 tbsp water
2 tbsp Date Paste (see p.108) or 2 Medjool dates, pitted

½ red onion, chopped
3 garlic cloves
2 tbsp fresh herbs (a combination of parsley and dill is best)
1 tbsp mixed dried herbs

Transfer the first 5 ingredients to a blender and blend to a cream on a high speed. You won't need to add more water if you have a powerful blender, but if your machine is struggling, add a little more water to help it along. Add the remaining ingredients and blend well. Transfer the mixture to an airtight container and refrigerate for up to 1 week.

Gravy

— SERVES 4

Traditionally, gravy is made with meat juices and fats, flour and refined sugar – not so nice when you think about it. If you still don't feel your meal is complete without it, try this plant-based alternative. It's seriously very good.

3 large portobello mushrooms, peeled and thinly sliced
¼ red onion
3 tbsp Soured Cream made with cashew nuts (see p.106)
2 tbsp apple cider vinegar

2 tbsp raw honey or agave nectar
1 tbsp raw tahini
3 garlic cloves, minced
pinch of Himalayan salt
4 tbsp warm water

Mix the ingredients in a bowl, cover and set aside for 4–8 hours to allow the mushrooms to marinate. Transfer to a blender and blend until smooth. Serve with any dish you wish to have with gravy – it's great with Creamy Cauliflower Mash (see p.102). Store, refrigerated, for up to 4 days.

Date Paste

— MAKES ENOUGH TO FILL A 500ML (18FL OZ) JAR

This paste is so easy to make and is a staple in my kitchen. Dates, being an excellent source of fibre, protein, magnesium, potassium, iron and calcium, make the most naturally nutritious sweetener for your meals, desserts, drinks, soups and sauces. This paste is used in many of the recipes in this book.

300g (10½oz) pitted dates

Pop all the dates into a jug or a large glass and just cover with water. Ensure you don't overfill with water – you only want the dates to soften for the blender and your digestion, not drown in water. Leave to soak for 6 hours, during which time you might like to give them a stir once.

Transfer the dates along with their soaking water to a blender and blend, using the tamper, until smooth.

Decant the paste into a glass jar with a lid and keep in refrigerated for up to 10 days.

Almond Butter

— MAKES ENOUGH TO FILL A 400ML (14FL OZ) JAR

With all their protein, calcium, vitamin E and antioxidant content, almonds are truly nourishing, alkalising and strengthening, and they taste so delicious, you might well think you've found nutty heaven. That is, until you taste almond butter! I can eat it straight from the jar by the spoonful. Just as well it's so simple to make.

350g (12oz) activated almonds or other favourite nuts or seeds (you can use unsoaked almonds, but if you soak them for 8 hours, then dehydrate for 40 hours, the nut butter you produce will be tastier and more digestible)
½ tsp Himalayan salt
80g (2¾oz) shop-bought nut butter or 4 tbsp extra virgin olive oil (optional)

Put the almonds and salt into the bowl of a food processor. Please don't attempt this recipe in a low-quality machine – to make a decent nut butter, you need a powerful food processor. Pulse until the nuts are broken down, then leave the motor running for 5 minutes. Scrape down the side of the bowl and allow the machine to rest for a few minutes.

If you would like a runnier end result, add the optional nut butter or oil at this point, then switch on the food processor and keep the motor running for a further 8 minutes. The result will be slightly chunkier than commercially bought almond butter.

Croûtons

— SERVES 4-6

Crunchy, flavoursome and seriously moreish, these croûtons are worth making in large batches as you can store them for weeks. They go well with salads and soups and are a little too easy to snack on.

120g (4¼oz) sunflower seeds, soaked for 4-6 hours
180g (6¼oz) almond meal (the pulp that is left after making almond milk, see p.33)
2 tomatoes, chopped
½ white onion, chopped
30g (1¼oz) dill
3 tbsp nutritional yeast
2 tbsp lemon juice
2 tbsp liquid aminos

Pop all the ingredients into a food processor with an S-blade and combine to a grainy paste. You may need to stop and scrape down the side of the bowl with a spatula from time to time.

Spread the mixture over a Teflex sheet to a thickness of approximately 1cm (½in). Dehydrate at 48°C for 10 hours.

Turn over onto a chopping board, peel off the Teflex sheet and cut into small squares. Transfer onto mesh trays and dehydrate for a further 20 hours.

Give the croûtons a crunch test – if they are perfectly dry, immediately place them in an airtight container and store for up to 6 weeks until ready to use.

Onion Bread

— SERVES 4-6

This raw, gluten-free bread makes all other breads envious. Take a bite and you might just consider becoming a full-time raw foodie. Make the ultimate sandwiches or serve this bread with soups.

120g (4¼oz) sunflower seeds, soaked for
   4-6 hours
100g (3oz) walnuts, soaked for
   4-6 hours
3 celery sticks, chopped
55g (2oz) raisins, soaked for 2-4 hours
1 red onion, chopped, plus ½ red onion,
   sliced thinly into rings
2 tsp caraway seeds, soaked in 1 tbsp
   water for 1 hour
2 tbsp ground coriander
1 tsp Himalayan salt
100g (3oz) ground flaxseeds, soaked in
   240ml (8¼fl oz) water for 1 hour
120ml (4fl oz) extra virgin olive oil
4 tbsp lemon juice

Put everything except the flaxseed, oil, lemon juice and sliced onion in a food processor and process to a paste. Add the remaining ingredients, excluding the onion slices, and pulse until well combined.

Halve the mixture and spread each portion over a Teflex sheet to a thickness of 5mm–1cm (¼–½in). Distribute the onion rings across the tops and gently press them in.

Dehydrate at 48°C for 10 hours. Turn over onto mesh trays, peel off the Teflex sheets and dehydrate for a further 10–15 hours, depending on the thickness of the bread. It is ready when it is dense and pliable and looks similar to the crust of a brown wholemeal bread loaf. Cut into slices of your desired size and store in an airtight container for up to 2 weeks.

Caramelised Onions

— SERVES 2

I never thought I could eat an onion ring, let alone an entire onion, in one go! Then I made this recipe and discovered a new love for onions. They have anti-inflammatory properties, contain lots of vitamin C, clean the blood and remove heavy metals from the body. So they're a good thing to love!

1 red onion
2 tbsp raw honey
1 tbsp tamari
1 tbsp apple cider vinegar

Peel the onion and slice it thinly on a mandoline. Combine the remaining ingredients in a bowl. Stir in the onion slices to coat them, then spread over a Teflex sheet and dehydrate at 48°C for 3 hours for a soft, noodle-like texture,

or for 10 hours for crispy rings – the longer you dehydrate the onions, the longer they will keep. Transfer to an airtight container. Store soft onions in the refrigerator and crispy onions in the pantry for up to 2 weeks.

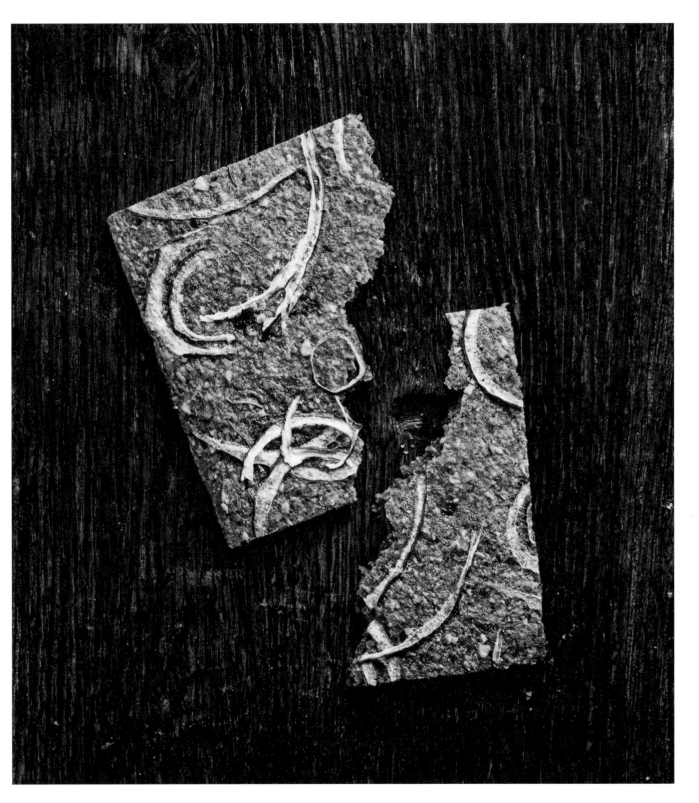

Onion Bread

CHAPTER 6

Desserts

How lucky we are to have a cuisine so pure,
nourishing and life enhancing that still has
sweet treats on its daily menu. Decadent living
desserts are precisely why raw food is not a diet
at all, although you'll always have my permission
to eat raw cakes for breakfast and tell
others you're on a diet.

Minty Chocolate Bark

— SERVES 1 (JUST KIDDING), AROUND 400G (14OZ)

At first, my raw diet was conditional: I will eat fresh, organic living vegetables, fruits, nuts, seeds and grains, *but* I will not give up my daily bar of chocolate. As my body purified and I began to feel healthier, my taste buds multiplied, cravings vanished and appreciation for quality soared. Commercial chocolate, with all its refined sugars, additives, processed dairy and preservatives, didn't quite cut it for me any more, so I looked for better alternatives. This chocolate treat will make you realise what I realised – that a raw food diet is not a diet at all.

130g (4½oz) cacao butter, grated
50g (1¾oz) cacao powder
3 tbsp agave nectar
½ tsp Himalayan salt

For the peppermint chocolate:
40g (1½oz) cashew nuts
1 tsp spirulina powder
2 tbsp lucuma powder
100g (3oz) cacao butter, grated
2 tbsp agave nectar
10 drops of peppermint essential oil
50g (1¾oz) pistachio nuts, roughly
  chopped

Line a large, shallow baking tray with kitchen foil.

Start with the dark chocolate recipe. Melt the cacao butter in a double boiler (or in a bowl set over a pan of gently simmering water, ensuring the base of the bowl does not touch the water below). Add the cacao powder and stir well until all the clumps are eliminated. Take the top pan (or bowl) off the heat and add the agave nectar and salt, stirring continuously.

Pour the melted chocolate over the prepared baking tray. Transfer to the refrigerator and leave to set for 5–10 minutes.

Clean the double boiler and use it (or the bowl-and-pan set up) to melt the cacao butter for the peppermint layer in the same way.

In a mini travel blender or nut grinder, grind the cashews, spirulina and lucuma together until the mixture turns to a powder. Add the cacao butter, agave nectar and peppermint oil and blend the mixture to a cream.

Pour this minty cream over the set dark chocolate slab. Sprinkle with the pistachios. Return to the refrigerator and leave to set for 10 minutes.

Using the back of a wooden spoon, break up the layered chocolate into shards, sized to your liking.

TANYA'S TOP TIP

You won't be able to taste the spirulina in this recipe, it is only there for colour. Feel free to substitute with chlorella, barley grass or wheat grass powders for a variation of green shades and nutrients.

Hazelnut Truffles

Hazelnut Truffles

— MAKES 20

Everyone deserves a good truffle in their lives. Make a batch of these divine morsels and they will keep in the refrigerator for up to eight months (which is just speculation; they never last that long).

200g (7oz) hazelnuts, soaked for
  6-8 hours and dehydrated at 48°C for
  40 hours to activate them
8 Medjool dates, pitted
50g (1¾oz) coconut oil, melted
2 tbsp maple syrup
1 tbsp tamari
2 tsp vanilla extract
50g (1¾oz) cacao powder, plus extra
  for dusting

Pulse the nuts in a food processor to the size you desire. I process them roughly so the truffles are packed with crunchy bits. For a creamy truffle, process for 10 minutes to a butter. Transfer to a bowl and set aside.

Process the dates, oil, maple syrup, tamari and vanilla in a food processor until smooth. Add the nuts and cacao powder and pulse to combine. Set in the refrigerator for at least 30 minutes.

Divide the mixture into 20 equal portions. Roll each one in your hands into a ball. Set on a tray, transfer to the refrigerator and leave to set for 1 hour, then dust with cacao powder (or put the powder in a plastic container with the balls and shake a little so they are evenly coated). If you want perfectly round balls, roll them again before dusting until their shapes even out. Store in the refrigerator.

Raw Chocolate Mousse

— SERVES 4

Sometimes, the most simple recipes are the most delicious, nutritious and nourishing. This treat is a favourite for athletes, breastfeeding mothers and those looking to improve their complexion.

2 ripe avocados
150g (5½oz) pitted dates, soaked
  for 4-6 hours
50g (1¾oz) cacao powder
1 tbsp coconut butter
1 tbsp vanilla extract
⅓ tsp Himalayan salt

Optional toppings:
berries, edible flowers, coconut flakes

Scoop the avocado flesh into a blender, add all the remaining ingredients, except the toppings, and blend the mixture on a high setting.

Divide the mixture between 4 dessert glasses, decorate with berries, edible flowers or coconut flakes and transfer to the refrigerator to chill for 2 hours before serving.

TANYA'S
TOP TIP

I've coached many athletes and I know just how much they enjoy a raw chocolate mousse, not only as a dessert, but also for breakfast or as a base to an afternoon milkshake.

Triple Chocolate Marble Cake

— SERVES 12

I always preferred using white cacao butter over brown cacao paste, as it gave me flexibility to create various flavours, colours and chocolate intensities. So I had a bag of cacao paste that had remained untouched for two years. I couldn't bring myself to throw it out, so I blended up all of it, only to discover the butterscotch layer of this decadent, delectable, indulgent bit of utter perfection.

For the brownie base:

110g (4oz) pecan nuts

150g (5½oz) hazelnuts

35g (1¼oz) gluten-free porridge oat flakes

50g (1¾oz) cacao powder

1 tsp Himalayan salt

450g (1lb) pitted dates, soaked for 4–6 hours only if too dry

2 tbsp maple syrup

For the chocolate butterscotch layer:

250g (9oz) cacao paste

130g (4½oz) cashew nuts, soaked for 4–6 hours

60g (2oz) coconut palm sugar

240ml (8¼fl oz) boiling water

½ tsp Himalayan salt

½ tsp butterscotch or caramel extract

For the marbling cream layer:

65g (2½oz) cashew nuts, soaked for 4–6 hours

105g (3½oz) coconut oil, melted

25g (1oz) xylitol

2 tbsp boiling water

2 tbsp lemon juice

1 tbsp vanilla extract

Make the brownie layer first. Grind all the ingredients, apart from the dates and maple syrup, in a food processor with an S-blade. Add the dates and maple syrup, then process again until well combined. Transfer the mixture to a 19cm (7½in) springform cake tin and press it down with your fist to cover the base.

Now for the chocolate butterscotch layer. Shave the cacao paste on a grater and melt it gently in a double boiler (or in a bowl set over a pan of gently simmering water, ensuring the base of the bowl does not touch the water below). Transfer the melted cacao paste and the remaining chocolate-layer ingredients to a high-powered blender and blend until smooth, using the tamper. Pour the mixture over the brownie base, scraping it all out of the blender jug. Before you wash the jug for the next step, you could add some nut milk (see p.33) and blend with the butterscotch layer remains (which are too good to waste!) to make a milkshake if you like.

Quickly put all the marbling layer ingredients into the clean blender jug and blend on a high speed setting. Now pour the mixture randomly in splashes over the entire cake and immediately insert a skewer into the layers to use it to draw swirls, being careful not to overdo it, so you marble the colours rather than blend them. Transfer to the refrigerator to set for a minimum of 3 hours.

For the marbling to extend through the cake layers (which looks good when sliced), hold the jug up high when pouring the cream and quickly move it lower and from side to side, so the cream penetrates the layers.

Strawberry Cheesecake

— *SERVES 12*

A couple visiting Tanya's Café had popped in for a teatime treat and went for this Strawberry Cheesecake. Within seconds, the lady ordered another slice so her husband could have his own, and was quizzing me about the cream and sugar we used in it, and for how long we baked it. She went on to tell me that she is a master at making cheesecakes, and never had she tasted one this delicious – and it involves no cheese, no refined sugar and most certainly no baking. What a compliment!

For the base layer:
150g (5½oz) pitted dates, soaked for
  4–6 hours only if too dry
115g (4oz) Brazil nuts
45g (1¾oz) desiccated coconut
⅓ tsp Himalayan salt

For the cream layer:
260g (9½oz) cashew nuts, soaked for
  4–6 hours
210g (7½oz) coconut oil, melted
120ml (4fl oz) lime juice (about
  2–3 limes)
140g (5oz) xylitol
2 tbsp vanilla extract

For the strawberry layer:
600g (1lb 5oz) fresh strawberries, hulled
5 Medjool dates, pitted
110g (4oz) agave nectar
1 tsp vanilla extract

Make the base layer first. Pulse all the ingredients in a food processor with an S-blade. Transfer the mixture into a 23cm (9in) springform cake tin and press it down firmly with your fist to form a crust across the base.

Blend all the cream layer ingredients in a high-powered blender to a smooth consistency. Pour the cream over the crust and refrigerate for a minimum of 3 hours to set.

To make the strawberry layer, place 200g (7oz) of the strawberries, along with the dates, agave and vanilla, into a blender and blend until smooth.

Cut the remaining strawberries into quarters, fold them in with the strawberry sauce and pour this chunky mixture over the set cake.

Remove the sprung side of the cake tin and transfer the cheesecake to a serving plate. The cake will freeze well for up to 2 months without the strawberry layer – simply make it fresh when you are ready to serve.

TANYA'S
TOP TIP

If you don't own a high-speed blender, you can still achieve a creamy cheesecake layer by adding 120ml (4fl oz) water to your blender.

Squashed Berry &
White Chocolate Cheesecake

— *SERVES 12*

I don't know about you, but I often find myself scraping every last bit of a cheesecake filling but leaving the crust. I decided it was time I made one without the crust and, for such a cake, what better combination is there than creamy, sweet, orangey white chocolate and soft, ripe, oozing, zesty berries?

For the cheesecake layer:
180g (6¼oz) cacao butter
260g (9½oz) cashew nuts, soaked for
  4–6 hours
120ml (4fl oz) boiling water
grated zest of 2 oranges
juice of 1 lemon
40g (1½oz) lucuma powder
110g (4oz) agave nectar
1 tbsp vanilla extract

For the berry topping:
220g (7¾oz) mixed frozen berries
  (I like a combination of raspberries,
  blueberries, blackberries and
  redcurrants)

Shave the cacao butter on a grater and melt it gently in a double boiler (or in a bowl set over a pan of gently simmering water, ensuring the base of the bowl does not touch the water below).

Transfer the melted butter to the jug of a high-powered blender, add the remaining cheesecake layer ingredients and blend, using a tamper, until creamy.

Cover the entire base of an 18cm (7in) round cake tin with the frozen berries and pour the blended cream all over the top. Gently rock the tin so that the cream spreads evenly between all the berries.

Refrigerate the cake for a minimum of 1 hour to set.

When you are ready to serve, run a small knife between the cake and the internal tin wall to loosen the cake. Place a serving dish face-down over the top of the tin, then flip over the tin and tip out the cake onto the serving dish.

Pick a heap of wild berries when they are in season and freeze what you don't eat. All berries freeze well for many months, so you can always have some to hand for making this delicious cake, even in the depths of winter.

Key Lime Pie

Pies

This Blueberry Pie is a favourite at Tanya's Café and has remained the number-one choice since the day we opened on 28 July 2014. There has only been one occasion on which we didn't serve it, when our organic supplier ran out of blueberries and, despite hopping on a Boris bike and cycling to half of London's organic grocers, I simply couldn't track down the sweet little things. As for the Key Lime Pie, I love limes, so, as they are not always easy to come by in winter, I squeeze the juice and freeze it in ice cube trays, which means I can have this pie any time of year.

Blueberry Pie

— SERVES 12

For the crust:
225g (8oz) pitted dates, soaked for
  4–6 hours only if too dry
100g (3oz) walnuts
45g (1¾oz) desiccated coconut
½ tsp Himalayan salt

For the filling:
300g (10½ oz) blueberries
150g (5½oz) cashew nuts, soaked for
  4–6 hours
105g (3½oz) coconut oil, melted
1 tbsp liquid stevia
1 tbsp vanilla powder
⅓ tsp Himalayan salt

Key Lime Pie

— SERVES 12

For the crust:
225g (8oz) pitted dates, soaked for
  4–6 hours only if too dry
100g (3oz) walnuts
45g (1¾oz) desiccated coconut
30g (1¼oz) cacao powder
1 tsp Himalayan salt

For the filling:
200g (7oz) cashew nuts, soaked for
  4–6 hours
240ml (8¼fl oz) lime juice (juice of about
  8 limes)
1½ ripe avocados
½ ripe mango
210g (7½oz) coconut oil, melted
110g (4oz) agave nectar

The method is the same for both types of pie:

Process all the crust ingredients in a food processor with an S-blade.

Transfer the mixture to a 23cm (9in) loose-based tart tin. Using your fist or a measuring cup, press the mixture evenly into the base of the tin and up the side.

To prepare the filling, blend all the ingredients in a high-speed blender on a high speed setting, using a tamper, or pulse in a basic blender, until smooth and creamy.

Pour the filling into your shaped crust and shake the tin a little to even out the coverage.

Refrigerate for a minimum of 3 hours to set.

Freeze these pies for a rainy day – they will keep in your freezer for up to 2 months. Defrost in the refrigerator, where they will keep for 2 weeks.

Honey Pear Walnut Cake

—SERVES 8

No trip back to New Zealand ends without me bringing home a bag full of high-factor manuka honey. Along with carrot juice and mint tea, it's the only food my body didn't reject when I was recovering from a car crash, with a very dangerously inflamed pancreas. This wonderfood is antiviral, antibacterial, antifungal and contains 22 amino acids, 27 minerals and 500 enzymes to soothe infections, treat skin issues, strengthen the immune system and aid digestion. Who would have thought cake could be so healthy? This one is perfect with a cup of fresh mint tea.

4 ripe Conference pears, cored

360g (12½oz) almond meal (the pulp that is left after making almond milk, see p.33)

100g (3oz) walnuts, soaked for 4–6 hours

2 ripe avocados

210g (7½oz) manuka honey (or any raw honey)

160g (5¾oz) coconut oil, melted

1 tbsp vanilla extract

½ tsp Himalayan salt

Chop 2 of the pears into small cubes, then chop 1 of the remaining pears roughly, to be blended up. Slice the last pear from the top to the base into 8 identical segments.

In a large bowl, stir the almond meal with the walnuts and the cubed pears.

Scoop out the avocado flesh and place it in a blender with the roughly chopped pear, the honey, coconut oil, vanilla and salt, then blend.

Carefully fold the blended ingredients into the almond meal mixture.

Spoon the mixture into a 19cm (7½in) springform cake tin and press down firmly with your hands to spread it evenly across the base.

Place the sliced pear segments on top of the cake in a sunshine-ray pattern, with the skin facing upwards and the thinnest part of pear pointing towards the centre of the cake.

Refrigerate for a minimum of 2 hours to set. Pass a fine knife around the edge of the cake to loosen it from the tin, then remove the sprung side of the cake tin. Don't worry if the cake crust begins to turn brown while the cake is in the refrigerator – it's natural, due to the high fruit content, and will only make your cake appear cooked. Store in the refrigerator at all times.

TANYA'S TOP TIP

If your cake tin doesn't have a loose base, line it with kitchen foil or greaseproof paper so that you can pull out the cake more easily.

From left: Chocolate Ice Cream, Coconut Vanilla Ice Cream, Mango Ice Cream

Ice Creams

When I make ice cream, I feel like a wizard! You can blend mango, banana or cantaloupe melon from frozen – it is simply revolutionary that a result so creamy can be possible with fruit and nothing else. My husband's favourite game was to ask guests to guess what's in my ice cream. Watching his face light up at their surprise that something so creamy had no milk, cream or sugar never got old.

Chocolate Ice Cream

—SERVES 2

2 ripe bananas
3 tbsp maple syrup
2 tbsp almond butter
2 tbsp cacao powder
½ tsp Himalayan salt

Peel the bananas and break them into 2.5cm (1in) chunks. Freeze for a minimum of 4 hours.

Put all the ingredients into the jug of a high-speed blender and process on a high speed setting, using a tamper, until the mixture is thick and creamy. Scoop the ice cream directly into bowls and serve immediately.

Coconut Vanilla Ice Cream

—SERVES 2

1 young Thai coconut
1 ripe banana
2 tbsp coconut butter
2 tbsp agave nectar
seeds from ½ vanilla pod

Open the coconut (see p.36), pour 80ml (3fl oz) of the coconut water into a cup and set aside in the refrigerator (you can refrigerate the rest to use in a juice). Scoop out all the white coconut flesh, clean it of any stone shards and roughly chop it into chunks.

Peel the banana and break it into 2.5cm (1in) chunks. Freeze alongside the coconut flesh for at least 4 hours.

Put the reserved chilled coconut water and all the other ingredients into the jug of a high-speed blender and blend on a high speed setting, using a tamper, until thick and creamy. Serve immediately.

Mango Ice Cream

—SERVES 2

1 large ripe mango
1 tsp vanilla extract

Optional:
2 tbsp cashew or macadamia nut butter
1 tbsp agave nectar

Peel the mango, discard the stone and chop the flesh into cubes. Freeze for a minimum of 4 hours.

Transfer the frozen mango to a high-powered blender. If your mango wasn't super sweet and ripe before freezing, add the nut butter and agave nectar before blending. Process on a high speed setting using a tamper. Serve immediately.

You can make ice creams from frozen fruit using a high-speed blender or a heavy-duty food processor. Creamier fruits, such as banana, mango, pear and cantaloupe melon, work best in ice cream recipes.

Carrot Cake

— SERVES 12

People often ask me if raw food is all about crunching carrot sticks. I can't help but giggle and reply, 'Nope, it's also about drinking carrot juice, applying grated carrot as a face mask and chewing carrot cake.' I do love my giant orange Vitamin A pills! I also really love this carrot cake and think you'll be pleasantly surprised at how similar its flavour is to the baked favourite.

For the cake:

150g (5½oz) pitted dates, soaked for 4–6 hours

70g (2½oz) dried pineapple, chopped small

750g (1lb 10½oz) carrots, grated and squeezed to remove excess liquid

50g (1¾oz) ground flaxseeds

60g (2oz) ground gluten-free porridge oat flakes

70g (2½oz) coconut oil, melted

75g (2¾oz) maple syrup

2 tsp mixed spice

1 tsp ground cinnamon

½ tsp Himalayan salt

For the icing:

1 vanilla pod

130g (4½oz) cashew nuts, soaked for 4–8 hours

50g (1¾oz) coconut oil, gently melted

80g (2¾oz) agave nectar

juice of 1 lemon

Prepare the cake layer first. Process the dates and pineapple in a food processor until the mixture becomes chutney-like.

Add the remaining ingredients and process again until well combined. Transfer the mixture to a 23cm (9in) springform cake tin and press it down firmly to spread it across the base.

To prepare the icing, scrape out the seeds from the vanilla pod. To do so, slice the pod in half lengthwise, then use a teaspoon to scrape out all the seeds until the inside of the pod is dry. Discard the pod.

Transfer all seeds and the remaining icing ingredients to a high-speed blender and blend on a high speed setting until thick and creamy.

Smooth the icing over the cake with a palette knife. Alternatively, if you prefer a runnier look, pour the icing over the cake, allowing it to drip down the side. Refrigerate the cake for 30 minutes to set the icing. Alternatively, if you prefer your icing to be runnier, remove the cake from the tin and pour the icing over it when serving.

The loose base of the cake tin is not completely flat, as it has raised edges. To remove the cake easily without losing any of it that may catch on this ridge, insert the base into the adjustable tin ring so that the ridge faces downwards.

Cupcakes

I wasn't quite doing the raw dance yet when Elliot and I relocated to London. After hearing friends rave about the Hummingbird Bakery on Portobello Road, we decided to visit it, and it was there that I first tasted a red velvet cake. Instantly, I knew I had to create a healthy version of this stupendously delicious dessert, and I'm very happy to share it with you here. And, of course, this book would not be complete without a chocolate cupcake. I would not be complete without a chocolate cupcake!

Red Velvet Cupcakes

— MAKES 8

For the cupcake mix:
140g (5oz) macadamia nuts
150g (5½oz) pitted dates, soaked
  for 4–6 hours
80ml (3fl oz) beetroot juice
1 tbsp lemon juice
180g (6¼oz) almond meal (the pulp
  that is left after making almond milk,
  see p.33)
3 tbsp cacao powder
3 tbsp powdered coconut palm sugar
1 tbsp vanilla powder (or the seeds of
  1 vanilla pod)
⅓ tsp Himalayan salt

For the icing:
1 quantity Carrot Cake icing (see p.130)

Optional decorations:
cacao nibs, rose petals

Chocolate Cupcakes

— MAKES 8

For the cupcake mix:
110g (4oz) pecan nuts
150g (5½oz) pitted dates, soaked for
  4–6 hours
1 ripe avocado
3 tbsp coconut oil, melted
180g (6¼oz) hazelnut meal (the pulp
  that is left after making hazelnut milk,
  see p.33)
30g (1¼oz) cacao powder
3 tbsp powdered coconut palm sugar
1 tbsp carob powder
1 tsp coffee extract (or 1 tbsp freshly
  ground coffee)
½ tsp Himalayan salt

For the chocolate icing:
1 quantity Raw Chocolate Mousse
  (see p.117)

The method is the same for both types of cupcake:

Process the nuts to a powder in a food processor with an S-blade, then add the next 3 cupcake ingredients and process again.

Add the remaining cupcake ingredients and process until well combined. You may need to stop and scrape down the edge of the bowl with a spatula a couple of times.

Form the mixture into 8 balls of equal size and place these into paper cupcake cases. Gently press down to give the balls flat top surfaces, to resemble baked muffins.

Scoop all the icing into a piping bag and squeeze it over the cakes. Refrigerate for a minimum of 1 hour to set.

TANYA'S
TOP TIP

If you make nut milk to produce the nut meal for these recipes, it will keep, refrigerated, for up to 4 days, and is delicious served with the cupcakes. Or use it to make superfood shakes. Alternatively, freeze it in ice cube trays to use in smoothies.

Tiramisu Pots

— SERVES 8

I'm really not a coffee drinker any more. In fact, just a sip of coffee makes me shaky for hours. That's until you mention a tiramisu. How double – and even triple – portions of this dessert don't have any effect on my stimulant receptors, I'll never know, but I'm pretty certain it's a case of all systems shutting off and finding any possible reason to enjoy my favourite treat in the whole world.

For the coffee cake layers:

140g (5oz) macadamia nuts

180g (6¼oz) hazelnut meal (the pulp that is left after making hazelnut milk, see p.33)

50g (1¾oz) ground gluten-free porridge oat flakes

25g (1oz) cacao powder, plus extra for sprinkling

300g (10½oz) pitted dates, soaked for 4–6 hours

240ml (8¼fl oz) espresso (30g/1¼oz ground coffee brewed with 240ml/ 8¼fl oz boiling water)

½ tsp Himalayan salt

For the vanilla cream layers:

90g (3oz) cacao butter, grated

130g (4½oz) cashew nuts, soaked for 4–6 hours

150g (5½oz) pine nuts

150ml (¼ pint) coconut cream (either the cream collected from 1 x 400g can refrigerated coconut milk, or made with 100g/3oz fresh young coconut meat)

120ml (4fl oz) hazelnut milk (see p.33)

150g (5½oz) maple syrup

2 tbsp sweet white miso paste

juice of ½ lemon

seeds from 1 vanilla pod

½ tsp Himalayan salt

To prepare the coffee cake mixture, process the first 4 ingredients in a food processor until finely ground. Add the dates, brewed coffee and salt and process again until you have a mixture resembling a runny, grainy cake dough. Set aside.

To prepare the vanilla cream layer, melt the cacao butter in a double boiler (or in a bowl set over a pan of gently simmering water, ensuring the base of the bowl does not touch the water below). Put the melted cacao butter along with the remaining vanilla cream layer ingredients in a high-powered blender and blend. Use a tamper to ensure that all the ingredients make contact with the blade and combine well into a cream.

You will need 8 small glasses or ice-cream sundae bowls, each with a capacity of 250ml/8½fl oz. Scoop

TANYA'S TOP TIP

1 tbsp coffee mix into each glass and spread it across the base. Set aside the remaining coffee-cake layer mixture for further layering later.

Pour in some vanilla cream until each glass is half-full. Set aside the remaining vanilla cream for further layering. Transfer the half-filled glasses to the freezer and leave to set for 1 hour.

The next step will have to be undertaken carefully, as the next layer of coffee-cake mixture could sink into the cream if you were to throw it on top. Simply scoop little bits of cake mix around the inside edges of your glasses, then add a bigger spoonful into the middle. Use the back of your spoon to lightly even out the surface, taking care not to apply any pressure.

Cover the cake layer with a layer of cream. Transfer to the refrigerator and leave to set overnight. Sprinkle with some cacao powder using a sieve and serve.

The tiramisu pots can be prepared well in advance, as they will keep in the refrigerator for up to 2 weeks. As the dessert infuses during refrigeration, the flavour becomes most pronounced after a minimum of 8 hours.

CHAPTER 7

Kids' Menu

Raw food isn't just for grown ups – kids love it,
too! Sometimes you may need to turn it into
a game, get the kids involved in the making
of their treats, spend a little longer sculpting
veggies into fun shapes or make healthy food a
reward to get them on board, but all you need is
a handful of go-to favourite recipes that have the
seal of approval from kids as young as two
to those in their 30s and 40s.

Falafels on Sticks & Minty Tzatziki Dip

— SERVES 6-8

All children are different and only you know which veggies your children will or won't eat. I know I loved mint as a kid but couldn't stand dill or, really, anything green and herby. But mint was delicious, because it wasn't a herb, it was summer! This dip offers a sneaky way of disguising the presence of dill while enjoying the minty flavours and summer memories. Dill has powerful benefits – it lowers blood sugar levels – and mint reduces the growth of bacteria and fungus in the body. Served on sticks, this dish is the perfect main meal for when the kids insist on eating in the sand pit!

1 quantity Falafels (see p.93)

For the minty tzatziki:
15g (½oz) mint leaves
240g (8½oz) Soured Cream made with cashew nuts (see p.106)
pinch of ground black pepper
150g (5½oz) grated cucumber
dill fronds, finely chopped, to taste

Combine the mint leaves, soured cream and pepper in a blender. Transfer the mixture to a bowl.

Fold the grated cucumber and chopped dill into the minty cream.

Cut 20 pretty paper straws in half and insert 1 into each falafel. Arrange the falafel sticks on a serving platter and serve with a bowl of the minty dip in the centre.

TANYA'S TOP TIP

If you want to go the extra mile with the fun factor, get the kids to select cookie cutter shapes they like and make falafel shapes instead of balls. Spread the falafel mixture on Teflex sheets to a thickness just shy of 2.5cm (1in) and get the kids to cut away. Combine the offcuts and cut again until the mixture is all used up. Then dehydrate as per the recipe on page 93.

Clockwise from top: Falafels on Sticks & Minty Tzatziki Dip, Coconut Jerky (see p.140), Mayo Pesto with Crunchy Veggies (see p.140), Rainbow Pizza (see p.141)

Mayo Pesto with Crunchy Veggies

— SERVES 3-4

Kids are much better than us at knowing what their bodies want and naturally go for creamy things, which are full of fats that are essential for healthy growth, and calories, for energy. For a raw food alternative to dairy dips, try this creamy, mayonnaise-like cashew dip – cashews are full of the essential fats and calories and also contain vitamins, minerals, fibre and phyto-chemicals that fight diseases. I serve this with seasonal crunchy vegetables, particularly mini veggies, which don't overwhelm.

For the mayo pesto:
50g (1¾oz) Pesto (see p.106)
120g (4¼oz) Soured Cream made with
   cashew nuts (see p.106)

For the veggies:
baby carrots, cherry tomatoes, radishes,
   cauliflower or broccoli florets, thin
   asparagus, sweet snowpeas, cos or
   romaine lettuce or baby corn

Stir the pesto and soured cream together in a bowl.

Slice up your chosen veggies, if they need slicing. Arrange them on a colourful plate with a bowl of mayo pesto in the centre.

Coconut Jerky

— SERVES 4

This is one of those recipes you should reach for if you've embraced the raw lifestyle but crave for meat. It came about as a happy accident – I had some coconut and date paste that were soon to expire, so I mixed them with spices and dehydrated the lot. I couldn't believe the result! We serve it as a bar snack at Tanya's Café and many customers take it away for their children's lunch boxes.

360g (12½oz) young coconut flesh
3 tbsp Date Paste (see p.108)
2 tbsp garam masala
2 tbsp tamari
1 tsp Himalayan salt

Scrape off any rough bits from the coconut flesh and slice it into long 1cm (½in) strips.

Transfer all the ingredients to a large bowl and stir them together using your hands.

Distribute the mixture over 2 Teflex sheets, ensuring the coconut strips aren't bunched together. Dehydrate at 48°C for 5 hours. Transfer onto mesh trays and dehydrate for another 5–15 hours, depending on whether you prefer the strips chewy or crunchy.

Rainbow Pizza

— SERVES 3-6

Not only does this pizza provide a fun way to get those evil veggies into your kiddies, presented in a colourful array of concentric circles, it also sneaks in protein- and fibre-rich coconut flour and flax, which are hidden in the gluten-free pizza base. If getting the kids to eat the vegetables is turning out to be too much of a task, make this vibrant pizza using fruits instead – with so much nutrition in the base, tomato ketchup and cashew cream anyway, they won't be missing out.

6 tbsp Ketchup (see p.107)
1 x pizza base (see p.86)
Cheese Sauce (see p.143) or Soured
  Cream (see p.106)
¼ quantity Coconut Jerky (see opposite
  page) (optional)

Rainbow veggie ideas:
Red: cherry tomatoes, red peppers,
  strawberries, red grapes
Orange: orange peppers, pumpkin,
  carrots, papaya
Yellow: pineapple, yellow peppers, sweet
  corn, yellow tomatoes, mango
Green: garden peas, snowpeas,
  asparagus, broccoli, kale, kiwi fruit,
  cucumber
Purple: beetroot, purple cabbage, red
  grapes, figs, blueberries
White: cauliflower, mushrooms, onions

Slice and chop your chosen veggies into tiny squares.

Spread the ketchup over the pizza base and drizzle with cheese sauce or soured cream.

Distribute the tiny veggie squares over the pizza in circular bands, ensuring that the largest band (the one that is next to the perimeter of the pizza) is made up of the vegetable or fruit your children like the best. Serve immediately. If you wish to serve the pizza warm, heat it in a dehydrator set to 48°C for 1 hour before serving it up.

TANYA'S
TOP TIP

If you don't own a dehydrator or can't manage to make the pizza base ahead of time, cook it in the oven. Follow the pizza base recipe on p.86, then spread the base mixture onto kitchen foil and bake it for 1 hour at 180°C (fan assisted). It won't be raw, but it'll still be the healthiest pizza your children are likely to eat.

Cheesy Spaghetti

— SERVES 2-4

I've been teaching this cheesy sauce recipe in my Raw Food 101 workshops since I started holding them in 2010 and I even demonstrate making it in my DVD. It's delicious, creamy and orangie-yellow in colour, resembling melted American cheese. I had no idea how many parents would write to me saying that they finally found a dairy cheese alternative that their kids actually like. Considering how not even one ingredient here is processed, bleached, refined, cooked or flavoured in a chemistry lab, I think that's pretty cool.

2 courgettes, peeled and spiralised

For the 'cheesy' sauce:
130g (4½oz) cashew nuts, soaked
  for 4–6 hours
120ml (4fl oz) hot water
½ red pepper, deseeded
2 tbsp lemon juice
25g (1oz) nutritional yeast
1 tbsp raw tahini
small slice of red onion
1 garlic clove
½ tsp Himalayan salt

Put all the sauce ingredients in a blender and combine using a high speed setting, using a tamper if needed. If you don't own a high-powered blender, you may need to add more water.

To warm up the courgette noodles, you can either steam them for 1 minute, dehydrate them at 48°C for 30 minutes or run hot water over them.

Stir the sauce into the warmed noodles and serve in tiny portions, so the meal seems accomplishable to your children and they ask for more. (So sneaky.)

TANYA'S
TOP TIP

My original sauce recipe can be found on page 176 – you'll notice the only difference is the quantity of nutritional yeast used. The Marigold brand product is enriched with vitamin B12, so for the kids' version of this sauce I cranked up the amount used, as this vitamin is hard to obtain in a plant-based cuisine.

Rainbow Veggie Wraps

— SERVES 4

Serving up a colourful veggie wrap is possibly the best way of getting an entire salad into your child without even trying. Kids don't like surprises when it comes to food, but they like food more when it looks like a surprise – wrap the meal in paper decorated with their favourite superheroes, attractive colours and eye-catching patterns and watch them enjoy unwrapping and eating the lot!

For the wrap:
2 medium courgettes, peeled and
  chopped
2 medium tomatoes, chopped
100g (3oz) ground flaxseeds
50g (1¾oz) walnuts, soaked for
  4–8 hours
juice of 1 lemon
4 tbsp extra virgin olive oil
½ tsp Himalayan salt

For the filling:
2 carrots
2 beetroots
2 green apples
2 ripe avocados
8 parsley sprigs
240g (8½oz) Cheesy Sauce (see p.143)
  or Soured Cream (see p.106)

Blend all the wrap ingredients to a paste, using your blender's tamper to ensure that there's always some of the mixture in contact with the blades.

Divide the mixture into 4 equal portions and spread each of these into round, thin tortilla shapes over Teflex sheets. Dehydrate at 48°C for 8 hours. Turn over the circles onto mesh sheets, peel off the Teflex sheets and dehydrate for a further 3–5 hours.

Scrub the carrots, beetroots and apples under running water – there's no need to peel them. Grate them on a grater or using a mandoline with the julienne blade inserted.

Cut the avocados into halves, remove the stones and slice the flesh while it is still in the skins. Scoop out the slices into a bowl.

Fill the centre of each wrap with layers of veggies and parsley sprigs. Give the veggies a coating of the cheesy sauce, then roll up the wraps and secure them with hemp string.

TANYA'S TOP TIP

If the wraps are not all eaten up, turn them into crackers. Cut them up with kitchen scissors and dehydrate at 48°C for 12 hours.

Pesto Crispies

Pesto Crispies

– MAKES 30-40 CRISPS

I published this recipe in my eBook *Nourished – Comforting Raw Foods for Winter* and was amazed by how many mothers wrote to say that their whole family loved the pesto crispies. And to ring the changes, you can make crispies using practically any leftover sauces and spreads.

2 courgettes
200g (7oz) Pesto (see p.106)

Slice the unpeeled courgettes into rounds on a mandoline. Spread the pesto over the slices, then assemble them on mesh trays. Dehydrate at 48°C for a minimum of 35 hours. Enjoy right away or store in an airtight container for up to 1 month.

TANYA'S TOP TIP

Set the mandoline to produce slices no thinner than 6mm (¼in), as the courgettes shrink dramatically in the dehydrator. Ensure they are no thicker than 1cm (½in), or they will take forever to dry.

Fruit Leathers

– EACH RECIPE MAKES 4 ROLLS

What kid doesn't like sweet, sour, aromatic and chewy fruit leathers? I remember often trying to swap my entire lunchbox at school for just one, with no luck! I'm glad now, as shop-bought fruit roll-ups contain many nasties. And so do many dried fruits, so when buying dates or apricots to make this and other recipes, check labels to ensure they contain no added glazing agents or preservatives.

For pineapple leathers:
½ ripe pineapple, shaved and chopped
  (about 350g/12oz without the skin)
10 dried apricots, soaked for 2–4 hours if
  too dry
2 kiwi fruits, peeled
seeds from ½ vanilla pod
½ tsp ground cinnamon

For watermelon leathers:
400g (14oz) peeled and chopped
  watermelon
130g (4½oz) strawberries, hulled
110g (4oz) raspberries
6 Medjool dates, pitted

Combine the ingredients for your chosen fruit leather flavour in a blender using a high speed setting. Pour the mixture over a Teflex sheet and spread it towards the edges, ensuring you don't make the layer too thin. Dehydrate at 48°C for 12 hours. Turn over the leather onto a mesh tray and carefully peel off the Teflex sheet. Dehydrate for a further 3–5 hours. Cut the sheet into 4 long strips, roll these into tubes and secure with hemp string.

Smoothie Ice Lollies

— *MAKES LOTS AND LOTS*

Use your child's favourite smoothies, cheesecake fillings, nut shakes or juices to make ice lollies. If you add layers of leftover smoothie mixes daily until the moulds are full, you'll have fun stripy lollies!

Ideas for kids' favourite flavours:
Tutti Fruity juice (see p.25)
Sweet Green Goddess Smoothie
  (see p.30)
Strawberries & Cream Smoothie
  (see p.31)
Choctastic Shake (see p.34)

Ideas for fruits to slice:
Strawberry, mango, kiwi fruit, cherry,
  star fruit

Peel, stone and cut the fruits into thin slices. Stick the slices onto the internal walls of the lolly moulds, then pour in the liquid – either to fill the mould, or to fill it part way, so you can make layered lollies. If filled, insert the lolly sticks and freeze. If layering, freeze for at least 4 hours, then repeat to add another layer(s), preferably with a drink of an attractively contrasting colour to the previous layer. Keep frozen until ready to serve.

If your mould has no lid to hold an inserted stick in place, wrap the opening of the filled mould with kitchen foil, then run your finger across the top to impress the outline of the mould opening in the foil. Use a small knife to pierce a slit in the centre of the foil. Insert the stick through this slit – the foil will hold it in place until the mixture is frozen.

Mango Custard with Strawberries

— *SERVES 2-3*

In Russia, my grandma would give me full-fat soured cream mixed with sugar, poured over fresh strawberries in a bowl bigger than my head – summertime heaven... In New Zealand, I discovered custard and Grandma got competition! This recipe reminds me of all the best childhood times.

150g (5½oz) almonds, soaked for
  6–8 hours
480ml (17fl oz) water
130g (4½oz) Date Paste (see p.108) or
  3 Medjool dates, pitted
1 ripe mango, peeled, stoned, cubed and
  frozen
3 tbsp lucuma powder
seeds from ½ vanilla pod
strawberries – many, many strawberries

To make an almond cream, blend the almonds and water, then strain, following the instructions for making nut milk on p.33.

Put 240ml (8¼fl oz) of the resulting almond cream, along with the date paste, mango, lucuma powder and vanilla seeds, into a blender and blend until creamy.

Chop, slice or dice the strawberries to your liking. Pour the custard cream over the strawberries to serve.

For a warm custard, do not freeze the cubed mango, and make the almond cream with warm water.

Smoothie Ice Lollies

Peanut Butter Cups

Nut-free Bliss Balls

— MAKES 25-30 BALLS

Little kids, big kids and 30-year-old kids all love a bliss ball – it's the perfect sweet snack. The benefits of mineral-rich coconut and its oils are extensive. These nut-free treats contain fibre, protein, iron and healthy fats, all vital for building and maintaining strong bones and tissues and for good digestion.

180g (6¼oz) desiccated coconut
150g (5½oz) pitted dates, soaked for
 4–6 hours
3 tbsp coconut oil, melted
2 tbsp maple syrup
1 tsp vanilla extract
20g (¾oz) freeze-dried strawberries or
 40g (1½oz) freeze-dried strawberry
 powder

Mix all the ingredients, except the freeze-dried strawberries, in a food processor until well combined. Then add the strawberries to the processor bowl and pulse to mix them in, ensuring they remain slightly chunky.

Spoon a little of the mixture into your hand and squeeze it to compress it, then roll it into a bite-sized ball. Repeat with the remaining mixture. Put the balls in an airtight container. Store in the refrigerator or in a cool, dark place.

Peanut Butter Cups

— MAKES 10

These beauties have been the biggest hit through my blog, my eBook of chocolate recipes, *Seduced*, and at Tanya's Café ever since the opening day. I had trouble working out which chapter of this book the recipe belongs in, but the joy on our mini customers' faces pointed to where it should go.

For the chocolate sauce:
60g (2oz) cacao butter, grated
70g (2½oz) coconut oil
4 tbsp cacao powder
1½ tbsp agave nectar or maple syrup
pinch of Himalayan salt

For the peanut balls:
130g (4½oz) peanut butter
15g (½oz) nutritional yeast
2 tbsp powdered coconut sugar
½ tsp Himalayan salt

Combine the peanut ball ingredients in a bowl, stir well, then transfer to the freezer for 1 hour to set. Divide the mixture into 10 equal portions or 15g (½oz) scoops. Roll each of these into a ball. If they start to melt, put them in the freezer for 30 minutes, then re-roll.

To make the chocolate sauce, melt the cacao butter along with the coconut oil, in a dehydrator set to 48°C or in

a double boiler (see p.114). Stir in the remaining chocolate sauce ingredients until well combined.

Half-fill 10 mini cup cases with the chocolate sauce. Carefully place a peanut ball on top of the sauce in the middle of each case. Refrigerate for a minimum of 15 minutes to set or until you are ready to serve.

Almond Butter & Jam Sandwiches

— MAKES AS MANY AS YOU LIKE!

Growing up in Russia and New Zealand, the closest I came to a peanut-butter-and-jam sandwich was via American TV. As a teenager, I lived in Hawaii and my childhood dream of biting into this classic American sandwich finally came true – a few too many times! I soon discovered that processed sugar-laden white bread, jam and peanut butter for three months straight do not produce the look of health. So here's a healthy raw version of this delicious combo for you to enjoy in a guilt-free fashion.

Muesli Bread (see p.49)
Almond Butter (see p.109)
Goji Jam (see p.46)

Spread, dip or spoon the almond butter and jam over slices of the bread and eat any way you like.

Chocolate Brownies

— MAKES 16 SQUARES

These brownies offer a stealthy way of adding calcium to your child's diet, as tahini (sesame) is a good plant-based source. For a burst of iron and chlorophyll, add chlorella or spirulina. That's the beauty of cacao – it's so good at disguising flavours. You can add nutritious algae and no one will ever know.

For the brownie base:
100g (3oz) walnuts
110g (4oz) pecan nuts
150g (5½oz) pitted dates, soaked for
 4–6 hours
2 tbsp raw tahini
50g (1¾oz) cacao powder
1 tsp chlorella or spirulina powder
 (optional)

For the chocolate icing:
50g (1¾oz) coconut oil
25g (1oz) cacao powder
1½ tbsp agave nectar or maple syrup
⅓ tsp Himalayan salt
raspberries (optional)

To make the brownie base, put the nuts into a food processor with an S-blade and process to a fine powder. Add the remaining brownie base ingredients and process until the mixture forms into a big sticky ball.

I use a 15 x 15cm (6 x 6in) square plastic food container in which to make the brownies, but you can use a baking tin or container of any size. Line it with a double layer of cling film, ensuring it overhangs the edges of the container so you can pull out the brownie easily once it has set. Scoop

the brownie base mixture into the lined tin and press down with your fist to compress it.

Melt the coconut oil in a dehydrator set to 48°C or in a double boiler (see p.114). Add the remaining icing ingredients, except the berries, and stir until all clumps are eliminated. Pour this sauce over the brownie base and top with raspberries, if using them.

Refrigerate for 30 minutes to 1 hour to set. Cut into bite-sized squares. Store refrigerated in an airtight container.

Clockwise from top left: Fruit Leathers (see p.147), Nut-free Bliss Balls (see p.151), Almond Butter & Jam Sandwiches, Chocolate Brownies

No-dehydrator Choc Chip Cookies

— SERVES 5

I know straight away if a recipe will be a great hit when I get my husband, Elliot, to taste test and he asks if he's allowed to finish it off. I always tell him to help himself but, with the odd recipe, I have to either remind him it's there or physically hand him the food. Not with these cookies, though... oh no! With these, he required no prompting or reminding – except to remember to leave some for me! And I suspect you will be reminding your kids to do just the same for you.

For the cookies:
130g (4½oz) cashew nuts
110g (4oz) raisins
45g (1¾oz) desiccated coconut
3 tbsp coconut oil, melted
2 tsp vanilla extract
¼ tsp Himalayan salt

For the chocolate chips:
50g (1¾oz) coconut oil
25g (1oz) cacao powder
1½ tbsp agave nectar or maple syrup
⅓ tsp Himalayan salt

To make the cookies, process the cashews in a food processor until broken down. Add the remaining cookie ingredients and process again until the mixture forms into a big sticky ball.

Divide up the mixture into 5 equal portions, form each of these into a ball. Press these flat on a Teflex sheet or baking paper. Use your fingers or a spatula to smooth out the edges of each cookie to give it a circular cookie shape.

To prepare the chocolate chips, start by melting the coconut oil in a dehydrator set to 48ºC or in a double boiler (or in a bowl set over a pan of gently simmering water, ensuring the base of the bowl does not touch the water below). Add the remaining chocolate chip ingredients and stir

well until all clumps are eliminated. Pour this mixture over a Teflex sheet or a sheet of kitchen foil. Transfer to the freezer and freeze for 10 minutes to set.

Once set, use the handle of a wooden spoon to break up the chocolate slab into chips of your desired size. Hold the handle perpendicular to the slab and crack the chocolate layer a few times. Then use a knife to cut the large shards into smaller pieces.

Press the chips into the cookies, ensuring you arrange them attractively across the surfaces of the cookies. Transfer your finished cookies to either the refrigerator or freezer and leave to set. They can be stored in the refrigerator for up to 1 month, and will keep for 3 months in the freezer.

Chocolate-coated Banana Pops

— MAKES 10 POPS

No one – and I mean no one – will ever get too old for this healthy treat. I love watching how much fun grown-ups on my retreats have when dipping, dunking and making a right mess with banana pops and their favourite sprinkles, so you can imagine what a perfect activity this is for kids.

For the ice cream:
5 overripe bananas

For the chocolate coating:
210g (7½oz) coconut oil, melted
50g (1¾oz) cacao powder
3 tbsp maple syrup or agave nectar
pinch of Himalayan salt

For the sprinkle dips:
Bee pollen, coconut, fresh berries, small
  grapes, freeze-dried fruits, goji berries,
  mulberries, golden berries, cacao nibs,
  dried rose petals, spirulina crunchies,
  hemp seeds, chopped nuts – go wild!

Peel and halve the bananas. Insert a wooden skewer or cake pop stick (a safer option for children) into the cut side of each banana half, inserting it at least half way into the fruit. Lay the pops on a tray and freeze for a minimum of 3 hours.

Cover the dining table with a tablecloth that's easy to clean or wipe. Put your chosen sprinkles into individual bowls or cupcake cases and place these on the table.

Mix the coating ingredients in a bowl and stir until all clumps are eliminated. Serve with the sprinkle dips. Kids can dip a frozen banana pop into the chocolate sauce, then immediately into their favourite sprinkles.

TANYA'S
TOP TIP

If the chocolate coating begins to harden, place the bowl inside a bowl containing a little hot water to melt the coating a little.

Rawtella

— FILLS A 500ML (18FL OZ) JAR

When asked what I missed most about cooked food, my answer was always 'Nutella' – until I created a raw version. The combination of hazelnuts and chocolate is a winner and kids go nuts for this one!

150g (5½oz) hazelnuts, soaked
  for 6–8 hours
65g (2¼oz) cashew nuts, soaked
  for 4–6 hours
105g (3½oz) coconut oil, melted
110g (4oz) agave nectar or 100g (3oz)
  maple syrup
2 tbsp cacao powder

2 tbsp hot water
1 tbsp extra virgin olive oil
1 tsp vanilla extract
½ tsp Himalayan salt

Break down the nuts in a powerful food processor. Add the remaining ingredients and process for a further 5–10 minutes until the mixture has your desired consistency. For a smooth mix, continue to blend in a powerful blender. Transfer to a jar and keep refrigerated for up to 2 weeks.

Chocolate-coated Banana Pops

CHAPTER 8

Party Food

One of my favourite things in the world is to
feed people. When I first moved into a shared
flat, I was ecstatic to be able to throw parties,
just for an excuse to cook up a storm and try
new recipes. Nothing much has changed since
going raw, except that I would uncook up a
storm. But the satisfaction levels have gone way
up, because now I can gather a room full of my
favourite people and offer them indulgent party
canapés, which are actually good for their health.

Superfood Cocktails

The debate on whether or not alcohol is harmful or beneficial is a complex one. However, if taken in moderation, using organic, vegan, gluten-free, top-quality spirits, mixing them with homemade juices and organic superfoods that counterbalance any adverse effects or possible hangovers, you can still socialise with your favourite tipple. These delicious cocktails go down well at any party!

Piña Colada

— SERVES 1

Give me anything that is Piña Colada flavoured and I won't say no, and if you hand over this cocktail, you'll have a friend for life. And I'm not just talking about me!

45ml (1½fl oz) light rum
120g (4¼oz) ripe pineapple, peeled and chopped, reserving leaves from the crown to garnish
90ml (3¼fl oz) fresh apple or pineapple juice (6 apples or 1 pineapple will usually produce enough juice for 4–6 servings)
2 tbsp coconut butter
2 tbsp manuka honey
handful of ice

Blend all the ingredients, except the ice and garnish, in a blender until creamy, then add the ice and blend again. Pour into a chilled highball glass or a goblet, garnish with the pineapple leaves and serve with a pretty straw.

Vodka Lavendade

— SERVES 1

A lovely, sophisticated drink, this lavender lemonade was inspired by my Californian bestie. I enjoy living a socialite life vicariously through her. When she texts me about the posh drinks she wishes were healthier, I'm already in my kitchen making them.

2 tbsp lavender flower buds
250ml (8½fl oz) hot water
45ml (1½fl oz) vodka
juice of 1 lemon
5 drops of liquid stevia or 3 tbsp raw honey
2 drops of vanilla extract
ice cube
sparkling water
lavender sprig, to garnish

Stir the lavender in the hot water and leave to cool, then strain. Pour 125ml (4fl oz) of the liquid into a champagne flute, add the vodka, lemon juice, sweetener and vanilla and stir together. Add the ice cube and stir a little more until the drink is chilled. Top with sparkling water and garnish with a sprig of lavender.

Mango Margarita

— SERVES 1

A classic Margarita is quite citrusy, and the great thing about that is the zingy flavour can be paired with your favourite fruit. My chosen blend is with mango, and once you taste this drink, it may just become your favourite, too.

¼ ripe mango, chopped, plus extra, cut into small cubes, to garnish
handful of ice cubes
70ml (2½fl oz) tequila/mescal
80ml (3fl oz) orange juice
juice of ½ lime
2 tbsp agave nectar
1 tbsp baobab powder

Muddle the chopped mango and some of the ice in a shaker (put the rest in a lowball glass). Add the remaining ingredients, except the garnish, and shake hard. Strain into the glass over the ice. Garnish with mango cubes.

From left: Vegan Sangria (see p.162), Mango Margarita, Vodka Lavendade, Frozen Acai Daiquiri (see p.162), Totally Tanya Mojito (see p.162)

Vegan Sangria

— SERVES 6

Although wine is made from grapes, the majority found on your supermarket shelves are not vegan. During the wine-making process, the liquid is filtered through animal-derived fining agents, including eggs, fish bladder, milk, gelatin, blood and bone marrow. Source organic vegan wine from a local supplier, add organic fruits and remind your guests how awesome you are.

40g (1½oz) coconut palm sugar
125ml (4fl oz) hot water
750ml (26fl oz) red wine (try a
   medium-bodied wine such as Rioja,
   Merlot or Malbec)
250ml (8½fl oz) orange juice
fruit slices (try apple, orange, pear,
   grapes, lemon and lime)
250ml (8½fl oz) sparkling water
ice cubes

Dissolve the coconut palm sugar in the hot water, then put the syrup, along with the other ingredients, except the sparkling water and ice, into a jug. Cover and leave in the refrigerator to infuse for 2–15 hours (the longer, the better).

When ready to serve, top up with sparkling water and pour over ice, distributing the fruit slices among all the glasses.

Frozen Acai Daiquiri

— SERVES 5

This drink is like a delicious slushy! It is so easy to garnish it and make it look beautiful. It's a must-have in the summer or the ideal palate cleanser at any time of year.

40g (1½oz) coconut palm sugar
125ml (4fl oz) hot water
250ml (8½fl oz) light rum
400g (14oz) strawberries, hulled and
   frozen
125ml (4fl oz) lime juice
1 tbsp acai powder
2 handfuls of ice
fresh berries, lime wheels or edible
   flowers, to garnish

Dissolve the coconut palm sugar in the hot water to create a syrup. Leave to cool. Put 150ml (¼ pint) of the syrup, along with the other ingredients, except the ice and garnish, into a blender and blend on a high setting until smooth. Add the ice and blend for a few seconds more. Pour into chilled martini glasses, garnish and serve immediately.

Totally Tanya Mojito

— SERVES 1

Zesty lime and cooling mint go so well together, it's hardly any wonder that the Mojito is a much-loved cocktail. I adore this combo, made with refreshing cucumber juice, so much that my sister made it for all of our wedding guests. And when we opened Tanya's Café, this cocktail was dubbed Totally Tanya on the menu!

½ lime, cut into 4 wedges
1 heaped tbsp coconut palm sugar
12 mint leaves, bruised
80ml (3fl oz) cucumber juice (a large
   cucumber produces 250–350ml
   (8½–12fl oz) juice, depending on
   your juicer)
45ml (1½fl oz) gin
ice
thin cucumber strip
sparkling water or kombucha

Put the lime wedges and sugar in a shaker and squash together with a wooden muddler. Add the bruised mint leaves, cucumber juice and gin. Fill the shaker with ice and shake hard. Stick a cucumber strip to the inside of a highball glass in a spiral, pour in the contents of the shaker and top up with sparkling water or kombucha.

Cheese Board

— SERVES 10

I don't think I've ever attended a Kiwi social event that didn't start with a cheese platter, so this book wouldn't be complete without a decent cheese board selection to kick off your party. Serve these tasty non-dairy 'cheeses' with Flaxseed Crackers (see p.179) and/or carrot and celery sticks.

For creamy cultured cheese:
130g (4½oz) cashew nuts, soaked for 4-6 hours
70g (2½oz) macadamia nuts
180ml (6fl oz) filtered water
2 tbsp lemon juice
powder from 2 probiotic capsules
½ tsp Himalayan salt

For herbed cheese logs:
1 quantity Creamy Cultured Cheese (see above)
your choice of coating mixture:
  ⅓ quantity coating mixture from Warming Avocado Fries (see p.102),
  ⅓ quantity coating mixture from BBQ Spiced Activated Nuts (see p.182),
  Italian herbs (mix 2 tbsp Italian herbs, 2 tbsp nutritional yeast, 1 tbsp garlic granules and 1 tsp Himalayan salt), or
  Detox Dust (mix 1 tbsp ground ginger, 1 tbsp ground cinnamon, ½ tsp ground cumin, 1 tbsp cardamom, ¼ tsp cayenne pepper and ¼ tsp Himalayan salt)

For pesto-layer cheese:
1 quantity Creamy Cultured Cheese (see above)
3 tbsp nutritional yeast
¼ quantity Pesto (see p.106)

For Cheddar cheese:
1 quantity quiche filling (see p.50)

To make the creamy cultured cheese, combine the ingredients in a blender on a high setting until creamy. Line a colander with a folded cheesecloth or a nut bag and scoop the mixture onto the cloth or into the nut bag. If using cheesecloth, fold the cloth edges over the mixture and turn over the parcel, ensuring no mixture can seep through the cloth edges. If using a nut bag, twist the loose ends to seal it, place the parcel inside another nut bag and twist to seal again. Position a small plate over the cheese in the colander and carefully put a weight on top. Place the colander on another plate to catch the 'whey', then set aside somewhere draught-free for 24–48 hours to allow the culturing process to take place. Serve, or transfer into a sealable jar and store, refrigerated, for up to 2 weeks.

To make herbed cheese logs, refrigerate the freshly prepared creamy cultured cheese for at least 2 hours to set. Use your hands (or roll it inside Teflex sheets) to shape it into logs of any size.

Choose a spice mix of your liking (I love them all, but the BBQ spice is something else!) and sprinkle it over a sheet of baking paper (you'll need as many sheets of paper as you have logs, and to distribute the spice mixture across the sheets). Roll each log in the spice mix on a sheet until none of the cheese is visible. Then wrap the paper around the log and refrigerate until ready to serve.

To make the pesto-layer cheese, line a large food presentation ring or a plastic food container with clingfilm so you can pull out the cheese when it has set. Mix the cultured cheese with the nutritional yeast. Spoon half the mixture into the presentation ring or plastic container to fill one-third of the container. Press down on the cheese with the back of a spoon to pack it tightly into the mould. Add the pesto until the container is two-thirds full. Fill the mould with the remaining cheese. Refrigerate for at least 2 hours until firm, then remove from the mould, slice and serve.

To make the Cheddar cheese, divide the mixture amongst 2–3 food presentation rings, ensuring the moulds are full. Refrigerate for at least 1 hour to set.

Upturn the rings over a mesh dehydrator tray and carefully remove the moulds. Dehydrate the shapes at 48°C for 20 hours. Refrigerate until ready to serve or for up to 10 days.

Summer Rolls with Sweet & Sour Dip

— MAKES 10-12

Everyone loves a good sweet and sour dip, especially when there are beautiful summer rolls to accompany it. There's no marinating or dehydrating time involved in making this party favourite, but you've got to get organised and work systematically. Rice paper wrappers can be tricky to play with and may require some practice at first. They are pretty cheap, so buy extra and remember to have fun with your rolling practice. The stunning results are worth the effort.

For the summer rolls:

selection of veggies (such as carrots, cucumbers, red peppers, asparagus, celery or bean sprouts) to produce approximately 800g (1lb 12oz) julienned veggies

selection of herbs and 20 edible flowers (such as parsley, basil and/or mint leaves, and pansies or other edible flowers)

lettuce leaves

12 rice paper wrappers (the ones I use are 22cm/8½in in diameter)

For the sweet & sour dip:

4 tbsp raw apple cider vinegar

4 tbsp agave nectar

4 sundried tomato halves in oil

juice of 1 lemon

2.5cm (1in) root ginger

1 tbsp tamari

100g (3oz) pineapple, chopped into tiny cubes

Julienne or slice your chosen veggies into thin, long strips. Set them out, along with the herbs and lettuce, within easy reach of a clean chopping board. Cover the chopping board with some sheets of kitchen paper.

Half-fill a bowl that is large enough to fit the rice paper wrappers with hot water. Dunk 1 wrapper into the water and keep it submerged until it is pliable. Then lay it on the kitchen paper on the chopping board.

Arrange 2 edible flowers or basil leaves, if using, face-down in a line across the middle of the wrapper. Top with veggies, selecting those with colours that contrast to the layer of herbs/flowers, for best visual effect. (Carrots over basil leaves, or cucumbers over purple pansies make the summer rolls pop!) Top with other vegetable strips and a line of herbs, ensuring you don't bunch them up in the middle of the wrapper.

Bring up the bottom edge of the wrapper tightly over the filling, then fold in the sides over it. Now roll up the wrapper, pushing the roll away from you, to completely seal the filling. Place the roll on a plate with the seam facing downwards.

Repeat the filling and rolling process with the remaining wrappers, veggies, herbs and flowers. Cover the rolls with lettuce leaves to keep them fresh while you prepare the dip.

Blend all the dip ingredients, except the pineapple cubes, in a mini travel blender. Pour the dip into a dipping bowl, sprinkle with the pineapple cubes and serve alongside the summer rolls.

Check out the homemade tea recipe on p.39 for ideas on which edible flowers you can use in these summer rolls.

Alkalising Cucumber Rolls

— *MAKES 10-12*

You don't often hear the words 'alkaline' and 'party' in the same sentence, but together we'll change the meaning of party to celebrate health! Treat your guests to these moreish cucumber rolls.

1 large cucumber
parsley sprigs, to garnish

For the filling:
150g (5½oz) almonds, soaked for
  6-8 hours
1 ripe avocado
juice of 1 lime
10g (¼oz) parsley
Himalayan salt and freshly ground black
  pepper

Using a mandoline, slice the cucumber lengthwise into long, thin strips.

Put all the filling ingredients in a food processor and combine to a chunky consistency.

Lay a cucumber strip on your work surface and spoon some filling onto the strip at one end, about 2.5cm (1in) in from that edge. Now lift up the end of the strip near to the filling, bend it over the filling and roll up the cucumber strip to enclose the filling, ensuring it doesn't fall out at the sides. If the cucumber strip is thin and pliable enough, it should stick together without support, but if it is not playing nice, use a cocktail stick to secure it. Repeat with the remaining cucumber and filling. Garnish and serve immediately, or serve chilled.

Sushi with Wasabi Dip

—*MAKES 12 SUSHI PIECES*

Wasabi and horseradish work miracles to fight off bacterial infection. Since food poisoning isn't uncommon at potlucks, this distinctively spicy dish is a pretty awesome immuniser to take with you.

2 x Nori Wraps (see p.94)
parsley sprigs or snowpea shoots,
  to garnish

For the wasabi dip:
240g (8½oz) Soured Cream (see p.106)
juice of 2 limes
2 tbsp agave nectar or raw liquid honey
2 tbsp water
2.5cm (1in) root ginger
1 tbsp wasabi powder

To prepare the sushi, cut each nori wrap into 6 equal pieces. Stand these upright on a platter and stick a sprig of parsley or some snowpea shoots into the centre of the top of each piece of sushi.

Stir together the wasabi dip ingredients and put the mixture into a serving bowl next to the sushi platter. Serve immediately.

TANYA'S
TOP TIP

If wasabi isn't your thing, I love love love this sushi with Ranch Dressing (see p.107). I know it sounds random but, believe me, it's divine, and is filling enough for a meal.

Alkalising Cucumber Rolls

Clockwise from top: marinating mushrooms for Portobello Sticks or Marinated Pesto-stuffed Mushrooms, Portobello Sticks, Almond Satay Dip

Portobello Sticks with Almond Satay Dip

— MAKES 8 SKEWERS

I knew I was on to a winner with this recipe when my husband, Elliot, and I threw a party and all his guy-friends wouldn't move away from the canapés table until these sticks and dip were all gone!

For the dippers:
400g (14oz) small portobello or chestnut mushrooms (ensure you have at least 24 caps)
1 quantity marinade (see recipe below)
1 large yellow pepper, deseeded and cut into 16 squares
8 cherry tomatoes, halved

For the almond satay sauce:
180ml (6fl oz) almond milk (see p.33)

2 tbsp Almond Butter (see p.109)
3 tbsp desiccated coconut or 2 tbsp coconut butter
2 tbsp tamari
2 tbsp toasted sesame seed oil
2 tbsp Date Paste (see p.108) or 2 Medjool dates, pitted
juice of ½ lime
2.5cm (1in) ginger root
¼ tsp cayenne pepper
1 garlic clove

Follow the recipe below to prepare and marinate the mushrooms. Spike the veggies onto medium skewers in the following order: mushroom/pepper/tomato/mushroom/pepper/tomato/mushroom. Place the skewers on a tray and refrigerate.

Blend all the sauce ingredients to a cream in a blender. Serve in a bowl alongside the skewers.

Marinated Pesto-stuffed Mushrooms

— SERVES 4 AS A SNACK

This recipe was my first ever savoury dish for YouTube. I remember having to stop myself from munching away on the yummy mushrooms so there would be some left to show in the video!

400g (14oz) medium chestnut mushrooms
½ quantity Pesto (see p.106)

For the marinade:
80ml (3fl oz) extra virgin olive oil
80ml (3fl oz) warm water
juice of 1 lemon
4 tbsp tamari
4 tbsp apple cider vinegar
2 garlic cloves, minced

To prep the mushrooms, carefully wiggle out the stems (do not discard the stems) and peel off the skins. Using a fork, gently pierce the surface across each mushroom and the stems.

Stir all the marinade ingredients in a baking tray, add the mushrooms and stems and shake gently to coat well with the marinade. Now turn the mushrooms so they sit like boats over the liquid with their gills facing up. Marinate at room temperature for 8–10 hours, shaking the tray from time to time.

Chop the mushroom stems and stir into the pesto. Spoon a little of this mixture into each mushroom cap, pressing it in to fill the opening.

Arrange on a serving platter and serve immediately, or refrigerate for up to 5 days.

Salted Caramel Slices

– MAKES 15

If there is a way to describe how divine these slices are, it won't be with words – it will be with sounds. But you won't hear me, as I'll be hiding in my room, hoping no one finds out what I've just made!

For the base:
130g (4½oz) cashew nuts
90g (3oz) desiccated coconut
150g (5½oz) pitted dates
1 tbsp coconut oil

For the caramel middle:
150g (5½oz) pitted dates, soaked for
  4–6 hours
105g (3½oz) coconut oil, melted
100g (3oz) maple syrup
240ml (8¼fl oz) hot water
1 tsp Himalayan salt
1 tbsp algarroba powder (optional)

For the chocolate icing:
50g (1¾oz) coconut oil, melted
25g (1oz) cacao powder
1½ tbsp maple syrup
⅓ tsp Himalayan salt

Line a 15 x 20cm (6 x 8in) plastic food container with a double layer of clingfilm, overlapping the edges.

Combine the base ingredients in a food processor with an S-blade until broken down. Transfer to the prepared container and press down to compress.

Process the caramel ingredients in a high-powered blender on a high speed setting, using a tamper, until creamy. Pour the cream over the base. Use a spatula to distribute it evenly across the top. Transfer to the freezer to set.

Stir the icing ingredients in a bowl until smooth. Pour the mixture over the caramel layer and smooth out the top. Freeze for at least 3 hours. Pull up the clingfilm to remove the block from the container. Slice into rectangles. Store, refrigerated, for up to 4 weeks.

Chocolate Fruit & Nut Clusters

– MAKES 20

With a Trail Mix ready to go (see p.180) and some cacao butter melted, preparing these takes no more than five minutes. So they're the ideal treat to whip up for a party, when there's already so much to do.

For the dark chocolate:
90g (3oz) cacao butter, grated
50g (1¾oz) cacao powder
2 tbsp agave or maple syrup
pinch of Himalayan salt

For the fruit and nut mix:
300g (10½oz) Personalised Trail Mix
  (see p.180), chopped

Put the cacao butter in a metal bowl in a switched-on dehydrator for 30–60 minutes. Or you can melt it in a double boiler (see p.114) or in a pre-warmed (but turned off) oven.

Whisk the melted cacao butter with the remaining chocolate ingredients until the clumps are eliminated and the sweetener doesn't sink. Pour the mixture over the trail mix and stir in.

Put spoonfuls of the mix onto a tray lined with baking paper, leaving room between each cluster. Refrigerate for at least 15 minutes or until serving.

Salted Caramel Slices

From left: Chocolate Fruit & Nut Clusters (see p.170), Piña Colada Roulade, Goji Berry Trifles

Piña Colada Roulade

– MAKES 10-12 SLICES

As far as I'm concerned, the best party begins and ends with a Piña-Colada-something. The coconut and pineapple combo is a close contender to strawberries and cream or mint and chocolate for me, but at a party, it always takes the cake! This recipe is easy to make but looks seriously impressive.

For the dark swirl:

135g (4¾oz) desiccated coconut
2 tbsp carob powder
160g (5¾oz) dried pineapple, soaked for 30 minutes if too dry
6 Medjool dates, pitted
2 tbsp Almond Butter (see p.109), or coconut butter for a nut-free version

For the white swirl:

240g (8½oz) coconut butter
80g (2¾oz) dried pineapple, chopped small

To make the dark swirl, blend the desiccated coconut and carob to a fine powder in a food processor. Add the remaining ingredients and pulse until combined into a big sticky ball. Spread the mixture very thinly over Teflex sheets to create a square.

To make the white swirl, first soften the coconut butter. Put it, in its glass jar, in a pot of hot water, or in a switched-on dehydrator for 30 minutes. Mix in the chopped pineapple, then spread the mixture over the dark swirl layer using a butter knife. Leave to cool.

Roll up the square carefully but firmly, pressing as you roll, slowly pulling the Teflex sheet away. Wrap the roll in clingfilm to keep it tight. Freeze overnight to set. Unwrap and cut into equally sized slices with an extra-sharp knife.

Goji Berry Trifles

– MAKES 12

These trifles are a stunning addition to any event. They also offer a great use for shot glasses, as well as an excuse for displaying seasonal flowers – and for making extra jam for the next day's breakfast.

For the base layer:

90g (3oz) almond meal (the pulp left after making almond milk, see p.33)
65g (2¼oz) hulled hemp seeds
40g (1½oz) coconut palm sugar
pinch of Himalayan salt

For the berry layer:

1 quantity Goji Jam (see p.46)

For the cream layer:

240g (8½oz) Soured Cream (see p.106)
80g (2¾oz) agave nectar
seeds from 1 vanilla pod

To garnish:

pomegranate seeds and seasonal flowers

Mix together the ingredients for the base layer and put the mixture into 12 shot glasses until one-third full. Top with a big spoonful of goji jam. Combine the cream layer ingredients and pour the mixture over the berry layer. Decorate with pomegranate seeds and flowers. These trifles will keep, refrigerated, for up to 1 week.

CHAPTER 9

On the Go

Many of the recipes in this book can be made in advance to have on the go, but it's within this chapter that you will find my favourite travel treats. They are easy to transport, can be stored for a good while and are easy to make – the perfect combination for an unforgettable trip. Choose your ideal travel companion from these tasty snacks.

Cheesy Kale Crisps

— FILLS 2 LITRE CONTAINER

I enjoy variety and get satisfaction from mixing things up and constantly updating recipes. There are just a few that have remained untouched since the first time I made them and these kale chips are one of those. To all my Virgo twins out there, I'd like to say that perfection is possible!

300g (10½oz) kale

For the 'cheesy' sauce:
130g (4½oz) cashew nuts, soaked for 4–6 hours
120ml (4fl oz) water
½ red pepper, deseeded
2 tbsp lemon juice
2 tbsp nutritional yeast
1 tbsp raw tahini
small slice of red onion
1 garlic clove
½ tsp Himalayan salt

Blend all the sauce ingredients in a blender on a high speed setting, using a tamper. If you don't own a high-powered blender, you may need to add more water.

Wash the kale, remove the stems and roughly chop the leaves into bite-sized pieces. Place the kale in a bowl and pour the cheesy sauce on top. Use your hands to massage the sauce all over the greens.

Arrange the kale over mesh trays and dehydrate at 48°C for 12 hours.

Store for up to 2 weeks in an airtight container or a zip-lock bag to keep the crisps crunchy.

Mock Tuna Sandwiches

— SERVES 4

Tuna causes acidity in the body, leading to skin issues, mood swings and tummy aches. This raw food take on a punchy tuna-mayo sandwich hits all the same flavour satisfaction buttons.

½ quantity Ranch Dressing (see p.107)
2 tbsp dulse seaweed
135g (5oz) pumpkin seeds, soaked for at least 1 hour
3 celery sticks, chopped
140g (5oz) green grapes, chopped
1 apple, grated
Onion bread (see p.110), Crackers (see p.179), collard leaves or nori sheets

Place the ranch dressing in a large bowl. Chop the dulse into tiny pieces with kitchen scissors and stir it into the ranch dressing. Now add the pumpkin seeds, celery, grapes and apple and stir.

Scoop a large helping of the salad onto onion bread, crackers, collards or nori to serve. The salad ingredients will keep for 1 week in the refrigerator, but it's best to put them together only when you're ready to eat.

Cheesy Kale Crisps

From left: Wasabi Crackers, Italian Flaxseed Crackers

Flaxseed Crackers

If raw food didn't include crackers, I would seriously have to rethink my view on it. When you transition to raw, you eat so many juicy fruits and veggies that you can crave for something crisp, chewy, dense and dry. It's this addiction to textures that makes it hard for many to stay on the raw wagon. These crackers really satisfy the yearning for crunch – you can bite them, dip them, lick them, spread on them, chew them and very easily overindulge in them.

Wasabi Crackers

— SERVES 8 AS A SNACK

150g (5½oz) whole flaxseeds
360ml (12¼fl oz) water
180g (6¼oz) almond meal (the pulp that is left after making almond milk, see p.33)
150g (5½oz) almonds, soaked for 6-8 hours
110g (4oz) dry buckwheat groats, soaked for 4 hours and rinsed well (see p.33)
2 medium tomatoes, chopped
juice of 2 lemons
4 tbsp wasabi powder
2 tbsp Himalayan salt
2 tbsp spirulina
2 tbsp agave nectar
2 tbsp extra virgin olive oil

Italian Flaxseed Crackers

— SERVES 8 AS A SNACK

300g (10½oz) whole flaxseeds
720ml (1¼ pints) water
240g (8½oz) sunflower seeds, soaked for 4-6 hours
30g (1¼oz) fresh basil
20 sundried tomato halves, soaked for 2 hours
4 medium tomatoes, roughly chopped
1 red pepper, deseeded and chopped
1 tbsp chia seeds
2 tbsp mixed Italian herbs
1 tbsp garlic powder
½ tsp Himalayan salt

The method is the same for both types of cracker:

Stir the flaxseeds with the water and leave to soak for 2-4 hours.

Put all the ingredients, except the soaking flax, in a food processor with an S-blade and process until the mixture resembles a thick soup. Add the flax and process to combine.

Divide the mixture into 2 portions and spread each over a Teflex sheet. Use a spatula to bring the mixture as close as you can to the edges of the sheet without it separating. Dehydrate at 48°C for 10 hours.

Place a mesh tray over 1 cracker and, holding the tray and the Teflex sheet together at each end, quickly invert the stack, then peel off the Teflex sheet. Repeat with the other cracker. Dehydrate on the trays at 48°C for 15 hours.

Chop up the large planks of cracker into equally sized squares and store them in an airtight container.

TANYA'S TOP TIP

Flax crackers can be of virtually any flavour. Play around with combinations – for instance, pick your favourite soup recipe, blend the raw ingredients and stir the soup with soaked flaxseeds and other nuts and seeds before dehydrating.

Veggie Crisps & Chews

— FILLS A 600ML JAR

These chews, the recipe for which was inspired by a friend I once ran a raw food market stall with, are my number-one travel snack. They're full of magnesium, calcium and amino acids.

For the vegetable chews:
2 medium carrots
1 parsnip
1 beetroot
1 sweet potato

For the spice mixture:
80ml (3fl oz) extra virgin olive oil
juice of ½ lemon
2 tsp dried rosemary
2 tsp ground black pepper
2 tsp Himalayan salt
1 tsp dried oregano
1 tsp dried thyme
1 tsp garlic powder

If you scrub the veggies in water, there's no need to peel them. Use a mandoline or the wide blade on a grater (a manual grater or a food processor attachment) to slice the veggies into thin, equally sized rounds.

Stir the spice mixture ingredients together, then pour the mix over the veggie slices. Use your hands to rub in the mixture to ensure all the slices get an even coating. Distribute the slices among 3 or more Teflex sheets and dehydrate at 48°C for 8 hours.

Transfer the slices to mesh trays and dehydrate for another 4 hours for chewy veggies, or 8 hours for crispy veggies. The slices will shrink to about a third of their original volume (so double or triple the recipe if you want a sizeable batch).

Enjoy the chews as they are, or serve with Ketchup (see p.107) or Ranch Dressing (see p.107).

Personalised Trail Mix

— SERVES 1 - YOU

A trail mix is the easiest snack to put together. It requires no effort, skill or special equipment, but it does call for a little imagination and a lot of personality in order to concoct your very own go-to burst of nutrition for whenever you feel peckish. Have fun creating your personalised version!

Here's a favourite combo of mine:
mulberries, goji berries, macadamia nuts, almonds, cacao nibs

And here's another favourite:
dried pineapple, golden berries, pumpkin seeds, coconut flakes, bee pollen

Ideas for additions:
dried mango, dried figs, dried apricots, dates, raisins, freeze-dried strawberries and other berries and fruits, spirulina crunchies/nibs, Cheesy Kale Chips (see p.176), broken Flaxseed Crackers (see p.179), walnuts, Brazil nuts, hemp seeds, sunflower seeds

Throw everything together in a large bowl, mix well and distribute among a few airtight containers to keep in your kitchen, office and/or car.

BBQ Spiced Activated Nuts

— FILLS A 1.5 LITRE (2¾ PINT) JAR

I first made these nuts for a supperclub and, once the café opened, they became a popular choice on our bar snacks menu. I keep a small bag on me most times, since snacking is my signature move!

For the nuts:
145g (5¼oz) mixed nuts and seeds (I use equal amounts of walnuts, Brazil nuts, almonds, hazelnuts and pumpkin seeds)
3 tbsp maple syrup or agave nectar
3 tbsp extra virgin olive oil

For the spice coating:
3 tbsp nutritional yeast
3 tbsp sweet smoked paprika
1½ tbsp coconut flour or buckwheat flour
1 tbsp mixed Italian herbs
1 tbsp garlic powder
1 tbsp ground coriander
1½ tbsp Himalayan salt

Soak the nuts and seeds overnight, then rinse them in clean water and drain thoroughly.

Transfer the nuts and seeds to a large plastic container, sprinkle with the maple syrup and oil, close the lid and shake the box.

Mix all the spice coating ingredients in a separate bowl, sprinkle them over the nuts and seeds, reseal lid and shake the container again a few times.

When you are satisfied that the nuts and seeds are evenly coated, transfer them onto Teflex sheets and dehydrate at 48°C for a minimum of 40 hours. Transfer to an airtight container, in which they will keep for up to 3 months if they remain in a cool, dry place.

Cinnamon Cookies

— MAKES 10-20

Cinnamon is a powerful anti-inflammatory – ideal for the bloating, puffiness and joint aches caused by flying. So now you have the perfect excuse to eat a cookie.

2 eating apples, peeled and chopped
75g (2¾oz) pitted dates, soaked for 4-6 hours
180g (6¼oz) almond meal (the pulp that is left after making almond milk, see p.33)
130g (4½oz) cashew nuts, soaked for 4-6 hours
3 tbsp coconut palm sugar
3 tbsp ground cinnamon
¼ tsp Himalayan salt

Put the apples and dates in a food processor and blend to a paste. Add the remaining ingredients and process to a grainy dough.

Transfer the mixture to a Teflex sheet, cover with another sheet and press down on the top sheet to smooth out the dough. When it is about 5mm (¼in) thick, peel off the top sheet. Stamp out biscuits using cookie cutters, leaving the offcuts intact.

Dehydrate at 48°C for 10 hours, turn over onto a mesh tray and dehydrate for 8-10 hours. Discard the offcuts.

Toffee Biscuits

— MAKES 8-12

My caramel obsession began in my grandma's kitchen. Knowing that I was coming to visit, she would boil a can of sweetened condensed milk for hours until the contents turned to gooey caramel heaven. I was her namesake and her baby daughter's first-born, so I probably could have got away with murder but, instead, was allowed to eat caramel straight from the can – it was our secret. The flavour of these biscuits takes me right back to Grandma's kitchen. They taste as sweet and as wonderfully naughty as those memories feel.

For the biscuits:

200g (7oz) walnuts, soaked for
  4-6 hours
150g (5½oz) hazelnuts, soaked for
  6-8 hours
100g (3oz) ground flaxseeds
90g (30oz) coconut palm sugar
2 tbsp algarroba powder
1 tbsp maca root powder
1 tsp ground cinnamon
1 tsp vanilla extract
½ tsp Himalayan salt
juice of 1 lemon
4 tbsp water

For the 'toffee':

150g (5½oz) pitted dates, soaked for
  4-6 hours
105g (3½oz) coconut oil, melted
40g (1½oz) coconut palm sugar
45g (1¾oz) algarroba powder

To make the biscuits, put the nuts in a food processor with an S-blade and process until fully ground. Add the remaining ingredients, except the lemon juice and water, and process to combine. Add the lemon juice and water, then process the batter to your desired consistency – a chunky mix produces textured biscuits, while a paste will give you smooth biscuits.

Spread the mixture over a Teflex sheet, evening it out with a spatula. Aim for a thickness of 5mm–1cm (¼–½in). Use a 7.5cm (3in) cookie cutter to stamp out biscuits.

Dehydrate the biscuits at 48°C for 12 hours. Turn the dough plank over onto a mesh sheet and place 1 or 2 mesh sheets over the biscuits to weigh them down so the edges don't curl up whilst drying. Return to the dehydrator for another 12 hours, then discard the offcuts.

Put the toffee ingredients in a high-powered blender and blend on a high setting, pressing with a tamper, to a smooth, sauce-like consistency.

Spread the toffee over each biscuit with a metal spatula. You can then eat them right away (you will want to, believe me!), or return them to the dehydrator for another 2–4 hours to make the toffee coating more dense. Or refrigerate for 1-2 hours to set, in which case, leave them there until serving or they will soften.

TANYA'S
TOP TIP

If you don't have a dehydrator or don't want to wait, you can also bake the biscuits in an oven. They will no longer be raw, but they'll still be the healthiest gluten-free biscuits you could get your hands on.

Clockwise from top: Granola Bars, Personalised Trail Mix (see p.180), Cinnamon Cookies (see p.182), Ginger Fudge

Granola Bars

— MAKES 12

When making granola bars, anything goes! You need two main elements – crunchy (nuts and seeds) and sweet and sticky (dried and fresh fruit). Try your own mixes, or make this favourite of mine.

150g (5½oz) dates, soaked for 4-6 hours
½ pineapple, peeled and chopped
1 apple, peeled and grated
1 tbsp ground cinnamon
1 tsp vanilla powder or extract
150g (5½oz) almonds, soaked for
   6-8 hours
135g (5oz) pumpkin seeds, soaked
   for 4-6 hours
60g (2oz) sunflower seeds, soaked for
   4-6 hours
45g (1¾oz) desiccated coconut
50g (1¾oz) gluten-free porridge oat flakes
3 tbsp chia seeds

Put the dates, pineapple, apple, cinnamon and vanilla in a food processor with an S-blade and process to combine in a creamy paste.

Add the almonds to the food processor and pulse until they appear roughly chopped. Add the remaining ingredients and continue pulsing until the mixture has your desired consistency – leave it chunky for crunchy bars, or break it down into a paste for softer bars.

Transfer the mixture onto a Teflex sheet and, using a spatula, mould it into a square with a thickness of 1cm (½in). Dehydrate at 48°C for 12 hours. Turn over the slab onto a mesh tray, cut into bars of your desired size and dehydrate for a further 20 hours. Store in an airtight container for up to 2 months.

Ginger Fudge

— MAKES 16 SQUARES

If you suffer from motion sickness, then it's ginger to the rescue! It's a star remedy for nausea. This ginger fudge is also packed with magnesium, calcium and amino acids, so you can't go wrong.

90g (3oz) cacao butter, grated
70g (2½oz) coconut oil
225g (8oz) pitted dates, soaked for
   4-6 hours
120g (4¼oz) sunflower seeds, soaked for
   4-6 hours
7.5cm (3in) root ginger (about 50g/1¾oz),
   grated

2 tbsp coconut palm sugar
1 tbsp Almond Butter (see p.109)
1 tbsp ground ginger

Melt the cacao butter (see p.114) and, once it starts to melt, add the oil. Blend in a high-powered blender with the other ingredients until creamy. Transfer to a lined 15 x 15cm (6 x 6in) container and level off the surface. Freeze for 3 hours. Pull out the block and cut it into 16 squares.

Superfood Glossary

Acai A berry, native to the Brazilian Amazon, that's potent in antioxidants. It is popular among athletes and is good for promoting healthy, glowing skin. Comes as a freeze-dried powder or frozen pulp.

Agave A sweet nectar that is extracted from the inner core of the cactus-like agave plant. Its true glycemic index and effect on blood sugar levels is a highly controversial topic, so use in moderation unless you know you have a reliable source.

Algarroba Ground seeds of a pod, also known as Peruvian carob or Mesquite meal. Full of protein and tastes much like toffee.

Baobab A dried fruit powder from an African tree, this nutrition powerhouse has a tangy, sweet, citrus-like taste.

Bee pollen Although a raw product and an ultimate superfood, bee pollen isn't considered vegan. Contains all nutrients for endurance, vitality, treating allergies and boosting your immune system.

Buckwheat Used as a grain, this is a gluten-free seed. Mild in taste and great if you want to add a crunch to dehydrated foods. High in protein, manganese and copper.

Cacao Available as a powder, butter, paste/liquor, beans and nibs, this is raw, real and unroasted chocolate, full of antioxidants and magnesium. All cacao products come from a bean. When cracked, it produces cacao nibs, and when stone ground, you get cacao paste or liquor. When the fat is extracted, it solidifies into cacao butter and what is left is the cacao powder.

Carob A distinctively dark and sweet powdered pod, some people use carob as a cacao alternative if they are sensitive to stimulants in chocolate.

Chaga Highly prized in Russian herbalism, this medicinal mushroom powder is a top superfood for immunity and has a simple earthy taste.

Chia A tiny but mighty seed that was once the survival ration of Aztec warriors. Contains amino acids, fibre, antioxidants and Omega 3s.

Chlorella A powder of dried single-celled, blue-green algae, full of protein, iron and chlorophyll, amazing for detoxing heavy metals.

Coconut flour An ideal alternative to wheat flour, it is packed with fibre and nutrients and has a very mild coconut taste. This powder is what remains after the oil is derived from shaved coconut flesh and dried completely.

Coconut water The freshest raw coconut water inside a young green coconut, coconut water is sweet, hydrating and full of electrolytes. Often mistaken for coconut milk, but they are two different products. Coconut water is transparent.

Cordyceps A medicinal fungus, traditionally grown on the bodies of caterpillars in China, this mushroom extract is now reproduced in laboratories without insects and sold as a powder. It's sweeter than most medicinal mushrooms, good for the heart, energy, performance and maintaining healthy cholesterol levels.

Dulse A purple-red sea vegetable, salty and slightly spicy, making it a popular choice for many dishes. High in iron and potassium.

Goji berry Delicious bright red berries, which are available to purchase dried, and have been used in Chinese medicine for over 6,000 years. Also called wolfberries, gojis are high in vitamin C, iron and selenium.

Golden berry A dried sweet, tart fruit, also known as physalis, cape gooseberry, Inca berry and Aztec berry. Energising and full of antioxidants.

Hemp seeds A seed with an earthy and nutty taste that's full of Omega 3s, protein and carbohydrates and free from any allergens.

Himalayan salt The highest grade of mineral pink salt, mined in the foothills of the Himalayan mountains in Pakistan.

Kelp noodles A raw spaghetti made from kelp, a brown seaweed that's high in iodine. Kelp noodles are tasteless, like rice noodles, so are perfect for bringing out your sauce or soup flavours. They contain no gluten, fat, cholesterol or sugar.

Kombucha A probiotic drink, also called 'living tea', because it is usually made by fermenting sugar and green tea with the help of a scoby (symbiotic culture of bacteria and yeast).

Liquid aminos Tastes and looks the same as a traditional soy sauce, but it's a wheat-free alternative. This protein-rich sauce is derived from soybeans, but isn't fermented, like tamari.

Lucuma A dried and powdered fruit from Peru with a subtle maple syrup aroma and sweetness. It is full of beta carotene. Traditionally, a more popular ice cream flavour than chocolate.

Maca Peruvians have been using this root vegetable for over 2,000 years as an energy enhancer. It's an adaptogen, a hormone balancer and a libido enhancer.

Matcha A bright green tea powder that's used in Japanese tea ceremonies and now all over the world to both energise and calm at once. It contains at least 100 times more antioxidants than standard green tea because it's shade-grown and you're ingesting the whole leaf.

Medicine flower Potent extracts derived from raw nuts, flowers and fruits, that contain no alcohol or preservatives. Used in uncooking, like food-grade essential oils.

Nori Best known because of sushi, nori is a Japanese name for edible seaweeds. They are shredded and dried into pliable papers, great for wraps, salad flakes and sushi.

Nutritional yeast Deactivated yeast, which is often fortified with vitamin B12, making it an ideal source of a vitamin that is difficult for vegans to obtain. Nutty and cheesy in flavour.

Probiotics Live cultures, available as powders or capsules, that are important for good digestion and healthy intestinal flora. Good for everyday use and especially after a course of antibiotics.

Reishi Since ancient times, the Reishi medicinal mushroom was reserved for emperors and royalty because of its longevity qualities. Still ranked as a number-one herb, it has a mild Bovril-like flavour and is great for relaxation.

Spirulina The most popular form of blue-green algae. Being 60 per cent protein, it is one of the best vegetarian sources of protein.

Stevia A sweetener that's 20 times sweeter than white sugar, stevia is the only truly healthy sweetener. It's safe for diabetics and contains an array of minerals. Comes as a powder of whole stevia leaves, but leaves an unattractive aftertaste, so look for a liquid extract that is dark in pigment.

Tamari A rich and delicious soy sauce that is made by fermentation, turning it into a healthy soy product. Tamari (or, alternatively, nama shoyu) is usually gluten free, but do check the label.

Wakame A sea vegetable that is soft and subtly sweet. An amazing source of magnesium, iodine, calcium and iron.

Wheatgrass Despite having 'wheat' in its name, this grass is gluten free, a potent detox agent and a blood purifier. Available as a powder of dried wheatgrass juice, which is full of all vitamins, minerals, amino acids and beneficial enzymes.

Yacon syrup A sweetener derived from tuberous roots of the yacon plant, native to the Andes mountains. The taste resembles caramelised sugar or molasses.

Xylitol Low-calorie sweet crystals that remain after evaporating birch tree sap. Looks and tastes very much like white sugar. Xylitol is the same stuff used in toothpastes, because it's safe for the teeth.

Meal Planning

Meal planning always seems time consuming – until you try it for a week and realise that you haven't had a week that awesome and satisfying in a while. A little organising can go a long way when it comes to better time management, taking the stress out of uncooking and falling in love with your kitchen all over again...

How to menu plan – step by step

1   Get yourself a stack of white cards for your recipes and a holder/folder to keep them tidy. Also, buy a wall planner or a calendar that has ample room for you to fit in three meal titles (one slot for each of breakfast, lunch and dinner).

2   Bookmark some good-looking recipes or Google 'raw/vegan/healthy dinner' ideas. (TIP: if you start gathering just two new recipes per week, by the end of the year, you'll have a collection of 104 favourite dishes to choose from!)

3   Use each card to record a single recipe. List the ingredients on one side and the cooking instructions, or the number of the page and title of the book that contains the recipe, for reference, on the other. (TIP: I split the ingredients list into two columns: fruit and veg in one column, nuts and condiments in the other, to save me time while supermarket section shopping. I also highlight any ingredients that require soaking or marinating to remind me to allow extra time).

4   On Sunday, flick through your cards and pick the dishes that get you most excited for the week ahead.

5   Know your staples, such as snacks, trail mix ingredients, favourite fruits and greens for juicing, sauces and pre-packaged dehydrated foods. I usually make Soured Cream made with cashew nuts (see p.106) and Ketchup (see p.107) on a Sunday for the week ahead, so I'll always keep the recipe cards for these dishes handy.

6   Fill out your weekly planner to ensure you have enough recipes for the entire week. Mark down on the planner all the times you plan to eat out and any busy days, so you can plan to have leftovers to use up. (TIP: If you want leftovers, establish whether or not you need to shop for double portions and make extra).

7   Scan over your chosen recipe cards and jot down all the ingredients you'll need to purchase for the week ahead. No time? Simply take the cards shopping with you.

8   Do whatever prep you can on a Sunday and check what needs soaking or marinating for the following day before going to bed. When you are ready to uncook, get out the relevant recipe card and gather all the ingredients listed on it before you begin any prep work.

Shops

Below I've listed some of my favourite places to shop – both online and local suppliers – websites I visit for amazing recipes and the latest advice on how to maintain optimum health, and books that continue to provide a fantastic source of daily inspiration.

For ingredients online:

detoxyourworld.com for medicinal mushroom powders, kelp noodles and organic nuts and superfoods

rawliving.eu for a wide selection of superfoods and ready-made raw products

buywholefoodsonline.co.uk for a great selection of organic herbs and spices

medicineflower.com for the best food-grade extracts

www.tree-harvest.com for nuts, seeds and cacao products in bulk

wheatgrass-uk.com for sprouting seeds, living sprouts and ready-made wheatgrass juice

For ingredients in shop:

Planet Organic for organic fresh produce, coconuts, spices, superfoods and probiotics

Whole Foods Market for nearly everything within this book

Waitrose supermarket for nuts, seeds, spices and a great selection of organic seasonal produce

Farmers' markets and local weekend stalls for fresh fruits, vegetables, greens and wild edibles

Local health shops for an ever-growing selection of superfoods, probiotics and often kelp noodles

For equipment:

betterraw.com/shop for my top recommended equipment for every stage of your raw journey

Resources

Good to know:

ewg.org information on pesticides and an up-to-date 'Clean Fifteen, Dirty Dozen' list

eattheseasons.com for a weekly list of seasonal foods

waterfootprint.org/en/resources for a snapshot of the impact of daily life, to help you reduce your water footprint

findaspring.com for your nearest spring water source

mercola.com for information on health-related issues

naturalnews.com for the latest news in the health world

mindbodygreen.com for inspirational tips and spiritual reading for diet, exercise and life

More recipes:

betterraw.com

rawmazing.com

thisrawsomeveganlife.com

therawtarian.com

therawchef.com

Favourite books:

Green for Life, Victoria Boutenko

12 Steps to Raw Foods, Victoria Boutenko

Going Raw, Judita Wignall

Raw Food for Dummies, Cherie Soria and Dan Ladermann

Superfoods, David Wolfe

RAWvolution, Matt Amsden

Thrive Fitness, Brendan Brazier

Raw Emotions, Angela Stokes

The Journey, Brandon Bays

Crazy Sexy Diet, Kris Carr

The China Study, T. Colin Campbell

Naked Chocolate, David Wolfe and Shazzie

The pH Miracle, Dr Robert O. Young and Shelley Redford Young

Holy Shift!, Robert Holden, PhD

Make Peace with Your Plate, Jess Ainscough

Healing Foods, Neal's Yard Remedies

Index

Acknowledgements

A hard-cover, full-colour recipe book was a dream of mine ever since I published my very first blog post back in 2010 and I'd often take a mental note of tips and recipes that would be perfect for a book. I was always a great believer in divine timing, so felt no rush. That is one of many spiritual lessons I took from Hay House, a publisher of some of the most influential authors, whose work, words and wisdom I treasure dearly. I can't even begin to express the gratitude I felt the day I signed a contract with this very publisher. *The Uncook Book* is a dream come true, not only because I got to work with such an amazing team, but because within its jacket is a collection of my best and most important work over the last six years.

THANK YOU SO MUCH TO
My soulmate, Elliot, the best sounding board, recipe taster, advice giver and supporter. You've been with me way before raw food was cool, were there through my diet, lifestyle and career changes, never complained about the blender going at 1am or that I stopped putting meat on your plate since 2010, and you still asked me to marry you.

My mum, dad and sister. You are my greatest cheerleaders, my inspiration, my motivation and my heart. I'm grateful for this family (and team) every single day.

Britney, for showing me what being a true friend means, for always being ready to help, for being my number 1 fan all over social media and for signing off every message with 'Love you'.

My editor Salima, for encouraging me not to worry about wordcounts and write freely even though it meant that she'd be stuck with the tough job of squeezing my pages of text into a paragraph. We've been on quite a journey together and I feel so lucky that it's been you.

Amy from Hay House, for believing in me and for staying true to your word that if Hay House UK were ever to publish a full-colour book, that you'd come to me first. You'll never know how much effect your kind and encouraging words had on producing this book.

Julie from Hay House for your bank of patience and your loving approach to everything you say and do. You are a true pro and working with you has been one of my biggest career highlights.

Leanne from Hay House, for so skilfully and enthusiastically collating everyone's demands for what would make a beautiful book and for being so good at keeping everyone in the loop at each stage of design.

Charlie, for your insanely amazing work, not just as a talented photographer on this stunning project, but my fellow food stylist, my trusty shoot-planner and a creative voice on how you envision the best recipe book to be.

My co-founders of Tanya's, Linda and Andreas, thank you for your support, encouragement and immediate blessing when I needed to step away from the café to finish the book.

Caroline from De Vallenger Design, for being the best shopping buddy and making me real pretty on shoot days.

Everyone at Tanya's Café, for helping me prepare, set up, move and wash up during shoots, without ever uttering a word of how much mess I can make in a short space of time.

Nikki and Christy from Hashtag Haute, for donating your adorable children for our kids section shoot.

My assistant and real-life angel/wizard/genie, Michelle, for being the most caring, loving and patient supporter throughout book writing and always.

You guys! This book is for you and because of you. It's impossible to put into words how much your cheering, curiosity, comments, requests, high-fives and stories have inspired me every step of the way.

Publisher's acknowledgements:
The publishers would like to thank Luana Gobbo for layout and design, Wendy Hobson for proofreading and Helen Snaith for the index.

Picture credits:
With thanks to the following for permission to use their images: 18L, Vitamix Total Nutrition Centre courtesy of www.vitamix.co.uk; 18CL, Tribest Green Star Elite juicer and 18R, Tribest Sedona dehydrator courtesy of www.tribest.co.uk; 18CR, Magimix Cuisine Système 5200XL courtesy of Magimix UK Ltd/www.magimix.uk.com. All other images © Charlie McKay/www.charliemckay.com.